101
GREAT
DATES

101 GREAT DATES

David D. Coleman
&
Diane J. Coleman

ABINGDON PRESS
Nashville

101 GREAT DATES

Copyright © 1995 by David D. Coleman and Diane J. Coleman

This book is printed on recycled, acid-free paper.

Library of Congress Cataloging-in-Publication Data

Coleman, David D., 1961–
    101 Great dates/David D. Coleman & Diane J. Coleman.
        p.   cm.
    Includes bibliographical references.
    ISBN 0-687-00775-5 (pbk.: acid-free paper)
    1. Dating (Social customs)—Miscellanea. I. Coleman, David D.
II Title.
HQ801.C66   1994
646.7/7—dc20   94-35288
                                                                    CIP

Cover & interior design by J.S.Laughbaum

95 96 97 98 99 00 01 02 03 04 — 10 9 8 7 6 5 4 3 2 1

MANUFACTURED IN THE UNITED STATES OF AMERICA

To
Shannon & Natalie
for the endless hours of love,
joy, and laughter you bring
to our lives

Contents

You Can Improve Your Social Life

Do any of the following excuses sound familiar? "I don't have time to spare." "There are just no good people left out there to date." "I'm too broke to date anyone right now!" "Why is it all the good ones are always taken?" "I just couldn't stand to go on another blind date." "I've been to so many movies that I could be a movie critic." "I'm just not ready for a relationship."

Generally, it is much easier for us to make excuses than to be assertive about making our social lives successful. With excuses, there is no risk involved and no opportunity for rejection. There is just simple rationalization and the inevitable loneliness that it brings. There are plenty of special people out there. Unfortunately, once we find someone we want to spend considerable time with, we rely on the traditional dates of frequenting a bar, going to a movie, going out for pizza, or dining at an extravagant restaurant. Then we wonder why our relationships fizzle.

What is a creative date? Dating creatively involves taking a bold, daring, spontaneous, and open approach to socializing. Go the extra mile for the person you are with to ensure that he or she has a good time and doesn't need to repay the kindness in some way. Go beyond the normal. Allow yourself to be spontaneous and romantic. Leave your personal dating "comfort zone." Take a calculated risk that the person you are with is looking for a change, and for something exciting and significantly different in his or her social life. Creative dating can be the spark that ignites a budding relationship. People appreciate extra effort and attempts to personalize dates. It's like receiving a handmade gift!

A simple definition of dating is, "spending meaningful, unique time with another person for the purpose of enjoyment and getting better acquainted in the hopes of spending more time with him or her in the future." A date does not always have to be serious, or preplanned, one-on-one, or take place within the comfort (or awkwardness) of a group setting. Dates do not have to cost a lot of money to be successful, nor do they have to take tremendous time and effort to implement.

Let's be honest. For many individuals, dating is a very stressful process. First, you must gain the attention of another person. Then, you must develop a plan for meeting the other person (that doesn't make you look foolish or desperate). Next, you try to find things in common. The date itself may include periods of forced, uncomfortable communication, deafening silence, personal disclosure, and probing investigations. Judgments will be made by both parties regarding the physical attractiveness, personality, intelligence, and character of the other person.

The purpose of writing this book is that it DOES matter and it SHOULD matter how, where, when, and why you spend time together! Your relationships can be exciting and full of special moments. This book will provide you with specific details on creative and out-of-the-ordinary dates to try. By using the principles in this book and by expending a little creative energy, you can have more positive and fulfilling relationships. You will feel less pressure while on a date and enjoy yourself more. Your dating partner will appreciate your thoughtfulness.

Quality relationships don't just happen; they take effort. No one else is going to do it for you, so the time is now. Get up, get out, and get moving. Quit watching relationships on television! Start working on your own. Give your social life a fighting chance. World-famous professional bodybuilder Rachel McLish may have said it best when she said, "Life is not measured by the breaths we take, rather it is measured by breathtaking moments." It is not how many dates you have, it is how enjoyable and original they are. Write the numbers from 1-101 on small slips of paper and place them in a large bowl. When you feel as if your relationship is in a rut and needs a jumpstart, pull out a card number and look up a date. Even if you don't actually use the idea, it may provide you with the motivation to be bold, take a risk, and be innovative.

1 Three Envelopes

The Essentials: Three three-by-five-inch index cards, three envelopes of any size (as long as they are not see-through), your car for transportation, and enough money to cover the "maximum" date chosen

The Date: Before picking up or meeting your date, design three potential dating ideas for that day or evening and write each one out on a three-by-five-inch index card. You could also be a bit sneaky and write out the same dating idea three times. Put a big number—1, 2, and 3—on the respective envelopes. Fasten them to the dashboard or window. When your date arrives in the car, he or she may select only one of the three envelopes. This will be your date for the day. Immediately rip up the other two envelopes and throw them away. This will drive your dating partner crazy as he or she will never know what dates were thrown away.

Then you carry out the date as seen on the card. If you want to be sure that you are in control of the situation and that it goes well, put the same idea on all three cards. Your partner will never know (unless you spill the beans) and will still believe that he or she controlled the destiny of the experience.

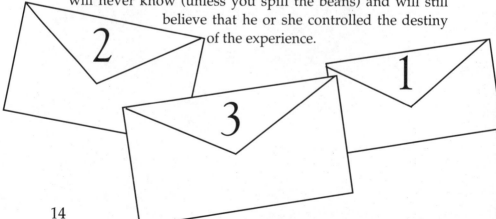

2 The Field of Dreams

The Essentials: A bag of popcorn and a bag of peanuts (with enough for two), comfortable and casual baseball fan attire, a blanket, a pair of binoculars, a Thermos full of your favorite beverage, and a noisemaker of some type

The Date: Why pay the high price of going to a major league baseball game when you can have just as much fun attending a little league game in your local community? Spread out your blanket and sit in a strategic location where you can cheer for both teams. Pay special attention to all the parents and other relatives who are watching their children play ball. The only drawback is that you'll probably have to throw back any foul balls you may grab. If the game gets a bit boring, turn on your radio to another game and pretend that you're there.

3 Revisit Your Childhood . . . Together!

The Essentials: Several coloring books and a set of 64 crayons, a jump rope, comfortable casual clothes, a cassette player with several children's tapes, a selection of Dr. Seuss books, a kite, chalk, a bubblemaker, a set of jacks, comic books, and a picnic lunch consisting of peanut butter and jelly sandwiches (with the crust cut off), two cans of Spaghetti O's (and a can opener), two apples, your favorite cookies, and a Thermos full of ice-cold milk

The Date: Go to an area where you can have some privacy and remember the feelings of joy and happiness you experienced as children. We seldom allow ourselves to have those same feelings as adults. Spread out a blanket and have lunch. Take turns reading the books to each other. Work cooperatively coloring in pictures. Lie on your back, look at the sky, and describe to each other what you see in the cloud shapes. Take the chalk to a paved area and draw a hopscotch board. Play jacks. Take turns outlining your silhouettes with chalk on the pavement. Do your best to get the kite in the air. Describe to each other your favorite memories of childhood and maybe even your most embarrassing moments. See who can blow the biggest bubble. For an added twist, visit each other's hometowns. Not only will this date be a tremendous amount of fun, it will teach you a great deal about each other.

4 Hunting with a Camera

The Essentials: A good 35mm camera (zoom lens if available), several rolls of color print or slide film, a picnic lunch, your favorite hunting dog (or just your own mutt), the proper and legal clothing necessary for hunting season, a knowledge of all rules and laws associated with hunting wild game, and a blanket

The Date: First, get all dressed up in your hunting garb, load your camera with the film of your choice, and head out to a large open field or woods and begin to "hunt" wild game. Go in search of rabbits, squirrels, pheasant, or deer—the type of animal doesn't matter. What does matter is that when you stumble across a wild animal, don't shoot it with a gun, but with a camera. It will be just as hard to get close to an animal with a camera as it is with a gun, because animals don't know the difference and can still see, smell, and sense you.

If you happen to see no animals at all that day, take pictures of each other, the landscape, your dog, whatever. Then, spread out the blanket (in a very safe, non-hunting area), get out the picnic lunch, and enjoy each other's company and the beautiful day.

5 "Just Married"

The Essentials: Empty soda cans, string, poster board, markers, dressy clothes, and a car

The Date: It's fun for a couple to fantasize about what it would be like to be married. Now you can at least experience the start of that adventure by pretending you've just stepped out of the wedding chapel, jumped into a waiting car, and are speeding off to some romantic honeymoon destination. (Don't carry this too far!) Pop in a tape recording of the Beach Boys song "Wouldn't It Be Nice," get a friend to chauffeur you around town, and for fun count the number of cars that honk at you in celebration. Each time you elicit a honk, smooch! Take advantage of the fun and enjoy the moment.

6 Fall Harvest

The Essentials: A pumpkin, a sharp carving knife (be very careful with it), candy corn, apple cider, art sticks, apples, caramels, two rakes, a small round candle, and about ten dollars

The Date: To begin with, each person takes a rake, and they head to opposite ends of a field or large yard (which is covered with fallen leaves). Rake the leaves toward each other so that when you eventually meet in the middle, you'll have a huge pile of leaves in which to frolic. Jump in the leaves, throw them at each other, and stuff large clumps down each other's shirts. Take a break and munch down some candy corn.

Next, head inside to the kitchen and melt down the caramels for caramel apples. While the caramels are melting (at a very low heat) the two of you place artwork on the pumpkin you wish to carve and then carefully, with the knife, sculpt the jack-o'-lantern. After that is accomplished, insert art sticks into the apples, dip your apples in the melted caramel, let them harden, and head for the nearest haunted house (thus the money).

7 Do We Have Similar Tastes?

The Essentials: A bridal registry worksheet from any major department store, a blank pad of paper, and the better part of a day

The Date: This date is for couples who have been dating awhile (several months) so that they know each other fairly well. Go to any large department store and ask for a blank bridal registry. Then, as a couple, walk around the store and pick out your favorite items as if you were soon to be married. The only catch is that you *must totally agree* on each item you choose for the registry: Flatware patterns, silverware, carving knives, glasses, fine china, and so on. This will give you a clear indication of each other's tastes and also your ability to compromise as a couple.

After you have completed the registry, head to the nearest furniture store and attempt to choose, as a couple, the furniture that you would place in your new home. Go room by room in your mind (living room, den, office, bedroom, kitchen, etc.) and, again, *you must agree!*

Barriers to Effective Relationships

Ideally, we all wish to be involved in a creative, romantic, and sensitive relationship with another person. Relationships often begin with one or both parties incorporating special, thoughtful, or spontaneous moments that endear them to their partner, and vice versa. When you feel that your relationship, be it brand new or long-term, is experiencing some difficulty, look for one or more of these barriers to effective relationships, and bring them forward for discussion. Possibly, by being frank, honest, and open, you can prevent the problems escalating to levels where they are relationship-threatening. Some barriers are:

* **Jealousy and Mistrust:** These cause people to question each other's loyalty and commitment. They cloud sensible thinking and place decision making in the heart rather than in the head. If people feel they are not trusted, it may lead to a self-fulfilling prophecy. Communication and understanding are the keys to overcoming these obstacles.

* **Possession Obsession vs. Mature Freedom:** This is characterized by one person's feeling that he or she now "controls" or "owns" the other person (I caught you and now you're mine!). This type must know everything about what the other person is doing, when, with whom, and why. He or she assumes that everything and everyone is a threat. For a relationship to be successful, both persons involved must feel that they have their own "space" and are allowed to maintain their individuality within the relationship.

* Allowing the Routine, Mundane, and Boring to Become Commonplace and Acceptable: Human beings are creatures of habit. It is easy for us to fall into ruts where we repeat the same behaviors. Nothing stymies a relationship faster than a lack of creativity. We always need to grow with and learn about our partner. When the spontaneity and passion disappear, so will the enjoyment.

* The Attempted Purchase of a Relationship: Money can buy good times, but it cannot buy love, a personality, a sense of humor, or a successful relationship. When one person spends a tremendous amount of money on another, it can throw a relationship out of balance and make the other person feel as if he or she now owes something or that expectations have been placed. Some of the most creative and loving ways of being together revolve not around money but around the fact that you will be spending time together.

* The Feeling That You Have Nothing in Common: If conversation and time spent together is a struggle, both parties will attempt to minimize the discomfort. Learn each other's likes and dislikes as quickly as possible. Learn about the aspects of life that your partner enjoys and become comfortable with them. Anything worthwhile in life is worth working hard to achieve.

* An Overemphasis on Finances: Financial inequities can strain relationships. If a lack of money between both parties is the problem, get creative. There are hundreds of fun and exciting ways to spend meaningful time together without spending a lot of money. Be flexible. Sometimes it is best just to pay one's own way.

* Pet Peeves Going Undiscussed: Agree to a standing rule that you will tell each other things that bother you right when they happen.

8 The Grandparent Interview

The Essentials: A small tape recorder with a working microphone, a few blank cassette tapes, and a prepared list of questions to ask your grandparents

The Date: Set up a time when the two of you can see each of your grandparents. They'll wonder what you're up to, but tell them you just want to visit. This date provides for four very positive outcomes to occur: (1) you will spend quality time with each of your grandparents; (2) they will enjoy seeing you; (3) you will leave with tapes full of memories that you will cherish in future years; (4) you and your date will know a lot more about each other's families.

On alternating dates, visit each other's grandparents. Turn on the tape recorder and begin talking with your grandparents (make sure it's okay to record their comments). Ask them fun, interesting, and humorous questions about their lives. How did they meet? Do they remember their first date? What is their fondest memory? What was it like when they were at the age you are at now? In years to come, the tapes will become precious to you. An enjoyable spin-off idea is to go on a double date following the interview. Maybe you'll go out for ice cream or for a walk through the park. Let the grandparents choose the activity and then go with them.

9 Babysit for Married Friends

The Essentials: Loads of patience, a few toys or games appropriate to the ages of the children you will babysit, a few healthy snacks, and your favorite video movie

The Date: Out of the blue, and with little forewarning, approach a married couple (with children) that you know very well and offer to babysit for them while they go out for a night on the town. At first, they will want you to undergo psychiatric testing, but will soon realize that you are sincere. "Married with children" couples really do need an occasional, guilt-free break. They will appreciate your enthusiasm.

Depending on how many children you're sitting for and their ages, it may take you awhile to get them ready for bed and asleep and to secure the household. But after this has been successfully accomplished, you will have time alone together to talk, snack, and enjoy one of your favorite movies (that is, assuming that the family has a television and a VCR).

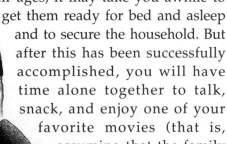

10 Tabloids Together!

The Essentials: A good sense of humor, the latest copies of several tabloid magazines (*The National Enquirer, The Sun Times, The Globe,* or *The Star*), and your favorite beverages and snack foods

The Date: This date is simple and inexpensive but could turn out to be a great deal of fun. Get comfortable (both in casual clothing and atmosphere), put on some of your favorite music, prepare your favorite snack foods and beverages, and then simply begin to read the tabloids together. In all probability, you will not believe your eyes. The stories are humorous, ridiculous, scary, thoughtful, and mindless. Your mind will run the gamut of emotions (and all for about 99 cents apiece), and you'll learn more about Liz Taylor, Michael Jackson, and aliens from outer space than you ever thought you would. Prepare to laugh harder than you have in a long while.

11 Three Wishes

The Essentials: Two index cards, two pens, a minimum of four hours of uninterrupted time, and each other's company!

The Date: Individually, take five minutes and write down three wishes that only your date can grant. These wishes should be realistic and achievable by your date, with minimal effort, right at that moment. The wishes should be reasonable and fall within the boundaries of good taste. They should not be designed to embarrass you or your dating partner. Additionally, the wishes should not cost an exorbitant amount of money.

One person's wish list should be completed before you move on to the next list. Wish list ideas are endless. You may wish for a backrub, help with your laundry, a special dinner, or for someone to simply give you some tender loving attention. The wishes are left up to your individual imaginations and creativity.

Progressive Dining

The Essentials: Your local Yellow Pages, the activities section from the most recent local newspaper, several hours of free time, and enough money for dinner for two

The Date: This date can happen in one of two ways, either by using letters of the alphabet or by courses of the meal. If you choose using the alphabet, you'll have your appetizers at a restaurant that has a name beginning with the letter A, your main course at a restaurant that begins with the letter B, and dessert at one that begins with a C (consult the Yellow Pages or newspaper to help you select places). The next time you go out, you would use D, E, and F.

If you decide to simply use courses of the meal, then just go to any restaurant for your appetizer, another for the main course, and a third for dessert. What is fun about using the alphabet is that you will probably end up trying a greater diversity of restaurants and food types as you discover new and exciting dining venues.

13 Volunteer Together

The Essentials: A car and an eagerness to help those less fortunate

The Date: One problem that many people face in relationships is that they feel a certain pressure to entertain each other and "make sure" that their date is having a good time. Volunteer dates can relieve all of that pressure, allow you to get to know each other quickly, and provide a service for others in need. You won't have time to think about yourselves—nor will you want to.

Many volunteer options exist within your local community. As a couple, adopt a grandparent at a local nursing home and visit him or her at least once a week. Just spending time with that person will brighten everyone's day. Volunteer for service at a local soup kitchen or homeless shelter. Volunteer to help take care of or exercise pets at an animal shelter or visit sick children at a children's hospital (and take them small, inexpensive gifts). You should first receive clearance from each of these agencies before going, but most will welcome your involvement. There will still be plenty of time after your volunteer effort to try out another date from this book if you so desire.

# 14 One-on-One Competitions

The Essentials: A basketball, checker board, backgammon board, Ping Pong paddles, bowling balls and shoes, badminton set, horseshoes, two putters, tennis racquets, golf clubs, shuffleboard equipment, and Frisbees

The Date: This date could take several days, months, or even years because it is a progressive and cumulative date. You and your date would play a series of one-on-one sports and games (that you mutually agree upon) and keep track of how well each person does. Don't worry that one of you might be a better athlete than the other; that is why handicapping exists.

The exciting part of this dating idea is the number of new sports and games you'll be exposed to and how much time you will be spending together. It is vital not to take the "competition" too seriously. Enjoy each other's company! You might also find a few sports that you really enjoy together and can play with other couples.

15 Everything You Do Starts with the Same Letter

The Essentials: A pad of paper and a pen, a baseball cap, the Yellow Pages, a current newspaper, several magazines, and two vivid imaginations

The Date: The premise of this date is simple: Choose one letter of the alphabet at random and brainstorm a number of activities to do that begin with that letter. First, tear a blank piece of paper into twenty-six squares. Label each from A to Z. Place them in a baseball cap, shake them up, and choose one. Then get out the pad of paper and start generating a list of activities that begin with that letter.

For example, if you select the letter S, potential ideas could be: sailing, skiing, making smores, sledding, sky diving, playing soccer, scribbling, snacking, squirting squirt guns, and so on. The possibilities are endless, depending on the letter you choose. When you run out of ideas, choose several from your list and carry them out. This dating idea can lead to twenty-six dates that are letter perfect!

A B C D E F G H I J K L

16 A TOUCH OF CLASS

The Essentials: Formal attire; a rented limousine; a red, yellow, pink, and white rose (one of each); reservations at your favorite restaurant, and a desire to be together for a night on the town

The Date: From time to time, it is a treat to have an extravagant night out on the town. So start now to save up a few bucks and treat yourself "royally" for an evening. Get nicely dressed, have a rented limousine pick you up and take you both to your favorite restaurant for dinner. Make sure that the roses are at the restaurant ahead of time and displayed on the table as you arrive. This shows thoughtful planning, and your date will be appreciative.

Next, move on to several of your favorite night spots for dancing and romancing. There will be no pressure to drive or find parking spaces, and you will feel very "special" for an evening. If you have some close friends that you would enjoy being around, invite them. This would also split some of the costs!

17 Scary Film Festival

The Essentials: The following movies rented on video (or laser disc if you're lucky enough to have one): *Psycho*, *Psycho II*, *Fatal Attraction*, *Cape Fear*, and *Final Analysis*, freshly made popcorn, casual clothing, comfortable furniture, blankets and pillows, and an assortment of sodas, candy bars, and snack food

The Date: This is a fun and inexpensive group date. If you are unattached, invite a bunch of your single friends (of both sexes) who want to meet others. If you are married or in a long-term relationship, invite several couples. Ask each of them to bring a specific item. Pop the popcorn, pass out the candy bars, and begin watching several of the scariest movies ever made.

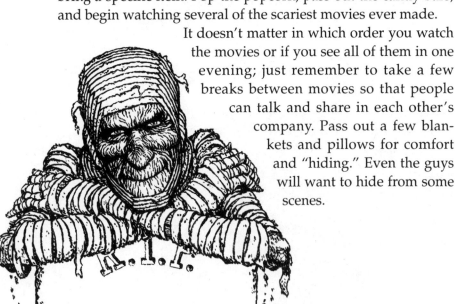

It doesn't matter in which order you watch the movies or if you see all of them in one evening; just remember to take a few breaks between movies so that people can talk and share in each other's company. Pass out a few blankets and pillows for comfort and "hiding." Even the guys will want to hide from some scenes.

18 *Beat the Heat*

The Essentials: A slip-n-slide, sprinkler unit, water balloons, hose (attached to a water source), a children's wading pool, Popsicles, a portable radio or tape deck, sunscreen lotion, and the ingredients to make delicious "mocktails" (non-alcoholic drinks)

The Date: Save this idea for the hottest, steamiest, muggiest day of the year. Put on your favorite music, throw on your bathing suits, and see who can slide the farthest on the slip-n-slide. Run through the sprinklers like you did as kids, throw water balloons, and hang out in the wading pool. Sip on a cool mocktail (maybe a "virgin" margarita or daiquiri) or slurp down a Popsicle. Lie out and let the sun and heat dry your body and do it all over again.

The mission here is to get cool and spend enjoyable, yet inexpensive, time together. This is an all-day date (or at least as long as the sun stays out or it stays hot!).

19 Make It, Spend It

The Essentials: All of your combined "junk" that you don't want (or need) anymore, a few tables, small stickers and a marker, a yard, garage or driveway, some starter cash ($20 in small bills and change), and a free day

The Date: Take all of each other's "junk" to one central location (either person's yard, driveway, or garage). Put stickers on each item and then write a "fair" price on it that you think will sell. Begin by pricing items a bit high so that you can come down and give the buyer a "bargain." Place a few signs and helium-filled balloons where passersby can see that you are having a sale. Your goal is to sell everything, so be flexible. The more cash you have, the more options you'll have later on.

At the end of the day, count up your earnings, choose another idea from this book, and celebrate your hard work!

20 Dare to Compare

The Essentials: About twenty index cards, two pens, and your favorite beverages and snacks

The Date: This dating idea provides you and your partner with an opportunity to get to know a great deal about each other's likes, dislikes, and "favorites" in life. Each of you takes several blank index cards and a pen. On separate cards, each of you will independently list your top five or ten favorite movies, songs, foods, pet peeves, books, actors, television shows, famous persons, and so forth. When you have each finished, trade cards and compare your lists. Examine what you have in common and where you totally differ. This exercise will provide you with great gift and dating ideas for the future.

21 High School Yearbooks, Baby Pictures, and Slide Show

The Essentials: High school yearbooks from each of you, as many baby pictures of each other as you can muster up (slides work well too!), comfortable clothing, and your favorite beverages and snacks

The Date: Begin by browsing through each other's yearbooks. Read the personal notes that your date's fellow classmates wrote. How much of what they wrote was right on the money and how much was not even close? Prepare to get in some hearty laughs at each other's expense.

Then, get out the baby pictures (or slides). This will give you an idea of what type of childhood you had, and it could be quite humorous. Don't overlook those special "blackmail" pictures (nudie baby photos or chubby pictures). Take time to talk about the favorite things you did as children and your fondest childhood memories.

Do's and *Don'ts* for Dating and Relationships

Do's

1. Watch less television. Instead of watching others' relationships, do something about your own.

2. Keep current. Be well read, keep current, and be able to hold an articulate conversation.

3. Keep fit. Remember that you have a mind, body, and spirit. Keep yourself mentally, physically, and spiritually healthy.

4. Be honest and sincere. This will be a refreshing change for many. Games and barriers waste time! Healthy relationships will not emerge from a false presentation of oneself to another.

5. Actively listen. Really hear what others are saying and react to what they have said. Avoid preparing your response while the other person is still speaking.

Don'ts

1. *Delay communication.* Every day you don't approach someone you're attracted to (and it doesn't have to be physical attraction) is a day he or she can meet someone else and possibly never know you.

2. *Pretend to be another.* Sooner or later you will lapse back into your "real" self and your date will notice.

3. *Dominate with "I" talk.* Let the other person learn about you, not hear about you. Let your actions tell who you are.

4. *Say what you think the other person wants to hear.* Let your true thoughts and feelings be known from the start. No facades.

5. *Fear the last five minutes of the date.* It is as awkward for the other person as it is for you. Be open and work through it together. Incorporate humor. Be honest with each other from the beginning.

Do think positively about yourself. You're a great catch! If you don't truly believe in yourself, who will?

22 Significant Places

The Essentials: A car or bicycles for transportation and a free day

The Date: This date is simple by design, but can reveal many qualities and interesting events of your date's life. Taking turns, each person chooses a location (within a reasonable driving or biking distance) that has significant memories from the past. Take your date to your chosen location, show him or her around the area and explain why that location is significant to you. What are your memories? What special event(s) happened there?

Choose two or three locations and then call it a day. If it has not taken too long, and you wish to spend more time together, choose another idea from this book and continue on with your date.

23 Personalized Coupon Books

The Essentials: Twenty slips of paper cut into equal lengths (or a small pad of blank paper), a pen, and a stapler

The Date: To begin, spend fifteen minutes talking with each other about personal likes and dislikes. From information you have learned about your dating partner and your conversations, prepare a ten-item coupon book for each other. Coupons may be redeemed one at a time and the dating partner must meet all requirements for each date. Using simple math, this activity could lead to twenty dates. Ten for each of you to redeem.

The coupons could be anything that your date would enjoy. A backrub, a trip to a masseuse, a night where you cook and do the dishes, a ride in the country in a convertible, etc. Make sure that if you design a coupon, you can provide the service!

24 Dare to Be Different

The Essentials: The needs could be different for each couple

The Date: Spend a day together where you take some calculated risks and attempt some activities that you wouldn't normally try. Get new hair styles. Eat dinner at breakfast time or breakfast at dinner time. Attempt something recreational even if you are not athletic. If you are athletic, try a sedentary activity. Learn to skydive, water-ski, or skeet shoot. Take a discovery course or camp out under the stars. Undertake whatever you two decide would be fun and a brand new activity for you both.

25 Do-It-Yourself Drive-in Movie

The Essentials: A portable television, two cloth or carpet squares, a VCR, two of your favorite movies on tape, an extension cord, popcorn, assorted sodas, assorted candies, and your car!

The Date: Drive-in movie theaters are becoming increasingly hard to find. Yet, going to an outdoor movie is still as much fun today as it was twenty-five years ago. So why stop? Clean up your car (inside and out) and park it in your driveway near your garage or a power outlet. "Fill" the backseat with popcorn, sodas, and candies. Put the cloth or carpet squares on the hood of your car (so you don't scratch your hood) and then place your portable television and VCR on top. Connect the VCR (armed with your favorite movie), wait for darkness to fall, then turn on your system. Adjust the volume so that you can hear easily, and you're at the drive-in!

26 Dash for a Date

The Essentials: A thirty-minute egg timer, three large bowls, paper cut into small pieces, and a marker

The Date: This is a great date for a group of single people. You invite all interested parties to a central location. Place the egg timer on thirty minutes. Each person in attendance has those thirty minutes to go out and find a date (or ask someone in the room) and get back into the room before the timer goes off. Once everyone is back and the time expires, each couple approaches the bowl that you have placed on a table. The bowl is filled with slips of paper with dating ideas on each slip.

The beauty of this date is that you can immediately go out and approach someone you've always wanted to date, explain your dilemma, and inquire whether this person is willing to help you out. If the answer is no, ask if a future date is a possibility. If the answer is no again, you're "toast" (but at least you know it). If it's yes, you're a happy person.

27 Car Cleanup Date

The Essentials: Car, cleaning supplies, roll of quarters, and plenty of "tunes" to work by

The Date: It's a proven fact (right?) that a car will drive better when it is sparkling clean and waxed—and proud of itself! At least your car will look better after you and a loved one share some work time together on this date and both of you will feel like you've accomplished something. Roll that vehicle into your neighborhood soft brush, do-it-yourself car wash and let the fun begin! On a hot day, don't be afraid to stand a little too close to the spray coming off the top of the car. There's always someone waiting for your spot so if there is time left on your wash, offer to spray down  the other guy's car too—a great way to meet people by being friendly and generous. Next, find a park and work on the fine details: windows, interior, and wax. While you're at it, check the tire pressure, fluid levels, and general well-being of your car.

28 Letter to the Editor

The Essentials: Computer or typewriter, paper and a writing utensil, address (where to submit letter), a topic of interest to you, and recent newspapers and magazines

The Date: If the last time you wrote a coherent paragraph was back in your freshman English class, get ready to brush up on your writing skills with this intellectual date. Browse through past editorial pages from the daily newspaper and get a feel for the issues being discussed. What is your opinion on these issues? Each person writes a rough draft and then shares his/her ideas. Be positive in critiquing each other's work. Next, prepare a final draft and send it off in an envelope to the paper. Who knows, you may get published! Instead of the newspaper, get your favorite magazine and look through the letters to the editor. Read these to each other for interest or just a laugh. You'll be surprised to find out how your date feels about certain issues and this may be a way to get to know each other better!

29 Ice Cream Machine

The Essentials: Ice cream maker, ingredients, elbow grease, friends armed with assorted toppings, bowls and spoons

The Date: Load in all those natural and delicious ingredients, grab that crank, and start churning! This is a favorite group date for you and several close friends with "sweet teeth." Make sure everyone brings their own toppings to share (assign them so duplication is avoided). The anticipation of freshly made ice cream will be almost unbearable as each person takes turns winding the crank. When it's ready, indulge! And the recipe will probably be some combination of the following: (Check your cookbooks or the instruction booklet of the ice cream maker.)

Ice
Flavoring (the fresh
fruit of your choice)
SUGAR!
Sweet cream
Salt

30 50s Flashback

The Essentials: Cheeseburgers and fries, jeans and T-shirts, music from the fifties, and a malt or milkshake with two straws

The Date: Take a step back in time by finding the nearest drive-in restaurant (these are making a comeback) and arrange to meet friends there. Wait a minute! Everyone must dress in fifties garb! White T-shirts, jeans with the cuffs rolled up, slick hair, bobbie socks, etc. Does anyone have a classic car from the period? Enjoy the cool evening air while listening to oldies over the speakers. Forget the lowfat diets today! Indulge in thick, juicy cheeseburgers and fries and top it all off with a shake. Continue the fun by going to the drive-in theater. None around? Try Date Number 25!

31 A Different Church Service

The Essentials: An open mind and appropriate dress

The Date: Take your date on an informative and spiritual date by attending a church service for a religious denomination other than your own. Check listings in the Saturday paper for the next day's services. There are as many different styles of worship as people, so expect to see some unique sights. This date may spark a conversation about religious values and beliefs, so be open-minded and sensitive to the other person's opinion. You will have the opportunity to meet many new and interesting people, and remember . . . you can invite them to your church as well. This date, if undertaken once a month, will provide you the opportunity to experience twelve different denominations.

32 Pet Shopping

The Essentials: A love of animals, some free time, and transportation to the pet store

The Date: If you've ever had a pet (and most people have), you know how special they become to their owners. If you are in the market for a pet, turn your search into a great date. Don't overlook the humane society or local pet shelter—often these animals are already housebroken and affordable. Also, if you are in the market for a dog and you live near a dog track, retired greyhounds are often for sale. They make great pets and you'll save a life! Some pet stores offer a service to match potential pets to people who would best be suited for that pet. After you've chosen that special new pet, select a name together. Remember to evenly share the duties of pet ownership!

33 *Strike a Pose and Smile*

The Essentials: A good 35mm camera, black and white film, tripod, mood music and boom box, and desired background setting

The Date: Having a good hair day? Take advantage of your good looks and the attention of your dating partner and take each other's picture. There's no fear of looking foolish when you know that only your date will see the crazy way you are posing. Make this a professional-style shoot complete with poses, different outfits, and backdrops. Quick— get back in time for that automatic timer to get a shot of the both of you! (A tripod may help here.) Really get into the action with some mood music playing on a boom box that you bring along. Say things like, "Work it baby!"; "The camera loves you!"; "That's a keeper!" Develop the pictures and create your own scrapbook of just the two of you! Who knows? Maybe one of the shots will make you both rich and famous. If this doesn't work, go to Glamour Shots.

34 Around the Campfire

The Essentials: Firepit and wood, starter kindling wood, newspaper pieces, matches, wieners and buns, smores ingredients (graham crackers, chocolate, large marshmallows), and a swiss army knife

The Date: Get ready for a night you won't forget! This date hinges on the ability to start a campfire in the middle of nowhere, so a little preparation would help (and maybe some fire starter fluid.) Once the flames are roaring, the hot coals will keep things burning. As your eyes get used to the night, you will probably notice raccoons and other critters moving in to steal the smores ingredients, so keep a lookout. This is a good time to share some scary stories with your date (who knows, this may cause your date to snuggle in closer from fear). There's nothing like the taste of a burnt wiener fresh off the flames! Slap some ketchup on and you're set. Note: follow safe practices in building your fire and completely extinguish it when finished!

35 The Hunt for Four-Leaf Clovers

The Essentials: A good set of eyes, a picnic lunch, and an open field.

The Date: Remember when you were a child gathering a bouquet of dandelions for your mom? On this date, you will get to experience that childhood excitement as you search for the ever-elusive four-leaf clover to present to your date. This time, however, you get all the pleasure as the first person to find one gets to hear the other person disclose four unknown tidbits about themselves. My lucky stars, this could get interesting! A twist could be, the finder gets four wishes from his/her date. After the festivities, a picnic lunch sounds great!

20 Barrier Busters!

If you are unsure of how to begin a conversation with some-one you don't know well, try a few of these barrier busters. Most people will have opinions to the following questions:

1. Describe a favorite place that you have visited.
2. Who makes you laugh more than anyone in the world?
3. If you could spend one day with anyone in history, whom would you choose?
4. Try some word associations.
5. What is your favorite television show? Movie? Actor? Actress?
6. Describe your idea of a perfect, romantic evening, from start to finish?
7. Describe your best friend from childhood. What did you most like about him or her?
8. If you could change one thing about yourself, what would it be?
9. What was the last thing you watched someone do that really impressed you?
10. What is your all-time favorite piece of clothing?
11. When was the last time you cried? Why?
12. What type of stations is your car radio programmed to?
13. What is the real and perceived you? Are they the same or different?
14. If you were casting a film about your life, who would play the main characters?
15. What would you put as the epitaph on your tombstone?
16. Do you have an in-y or out-y belly button?
17. What do you do to chill-out and relieve stress?
18. What are a few of your pet peeves?
19. Can you do a really good imitation of anyone or anything?
20. What is your first impression of me . . . be honest.

36 Clothes That Clash

The Essentials: Guts, clashing or outlandish clothes, and a great sense of humor

The Date: You will certainly leave your comfort zone on this date. You and your date must dress in the most outlandish and flamboyant clothes that you can find and actually go out in public dressed this way. Shopping at thrift stores is essential to the success of this date (and your wallets). The key is to act as if nothing is awry. Most of your enjoyment on this date will be watching other people's reactions. Play it for all it's worth! Depending on where you go, you might just be the norm!

37 The Romantic Recording

The Essentials: A good quality audio system for taping from tape-to-tape or compact disc to tape, blank tape, and a diverse collection of music

The Date: Nothing evokes emotions and memories quite like music. Let music express to your date those thoughts that you have but can't quite vocalize. Often, a certain song will become the theme song for your relationship. Whatever the effect, have fun thinking about your friend while jamming to your favorite tunes. The tape case itself can be personalized with a title for your tape or even a picture drawn by you. Your dating partner will be thrilled and impressed if you can create a tape full of songs that appeals to his or her tastes.

38 Rainstorm Rendezvous

The Essentials: Safe and comfortable shelter, an umbrella (preferably not a steel shaft), and inclement weather!

The Date: You can smell it—a storm is brewing outside. The wind is whipping up, leaves are turning over, and there is a certain excitement in the air. Arrange to watch the storm with your favorite date. Find safe shelter (especially if the storm is accompanied by lightning) and park yourself on some comfortable lawn chairs for the duration. Calculate the distance of the storm by counting "One thousand one, one thousand two . . ." after the lightning flashes and listen for the thunder (one second for every mile away). Watch as the worms mysteriously crawl out onto the wet pavement. Share stories about how your parents tried to console you with tales of "Oh, don't be afraid of the storm, it's just God up there bowling!" After the storm passes, take a walk or a drive and breathe in the fresh air!

39 Who, Me... Juggle?

The Essentials: Klutz juggling book and accompanying juggling bags, patience, and a great sense of humor

The Date: Learning to juggle is easier than you think. To find out more about the character and stick-to-it-iveness of your date, challenge him or her to learn to juggle with you. You will be rolling on the floor laughing as you try to master the steps. Take turns picking up after each other and remember to be positive. Decide at the start—"WE WILL DO THIS!" If there is one available, get out and watch a real juggler in action; then treat yourselves to an ice cream cone.

Pizza from Scratch

The Essentials: Pizza ingredients, chef hats and aprons, pail of water, mop, and a well-equipped kitchen

The Date: This date will take teamwork and a sense of humor. Start by getting decked-out in baking gear (aprons and hats). Practice talking to each other with ethnic accents. Gather all ingredients and dive in! Here is a simple dough recipe to begin:

PIZZA DOUGH

1 package active dry yeast	1 teaspoon salt
1 cup warm water	2 tablespoons vegetable oil
1 teaspoon sugar	2 1/2 cups all-purpose flour

Dissolve yeast in warm water. Stir in remaining ingredients; beat vigorously 20 strokes. Let rest about 5 minutes.

After the dough is prepared, the sauce and toppings are all up to you! To add spice to this date, invite a bunch of friends and ask each one to bring a specific pizza topping. If you want, throw any movie starring Al Pacino into the VCR and call it an evening.

41 Back-of-the Cupboards Dinner

The Essentials: Any food package or items found at the back of the cupboard (or refrigerator) that are still edible

The Date: Test your resourcefulness (and stomach lining) by putting together a delicious feast using only those items found in the dark recesses of your cupboards and refrigerator. A can of tuna fish? Yea! A package of Chinese noodles? Great! Creamed corn? Cool! (Anything that is actually MOVING should not be used!) You will be amazed at how resourceful you can be when you're both hungry. To prepare a tasty dish will also force you to cooperate.

 Formal Fast-Food Dinner

The Essentials: Formal place setting complete with silverware, cloth napkins, tablecloth, flowers, candles, crystal

The Date: Get ready to turn some heads with this one. Again, the key to this date is to act as if nothing is awry. Get nicely dressed up: a coat and tie for the man and a dress or suit for the woman. Head to a fast-food restaurant and select a booth or table. Take a few minutes to set up a beautiful dining area for two. Then, one of you go to the counter, order, and then serve the other. Do the same thing for dessert (only head to another place). If they are willing, invite another couple and double-date. Maybe a good friend will act as a waiter or waitress for you.

43 Elvis Party

The Essentials: A camera, assorted Elvis movies, pictures, tapes or CDs, peanut butter, bologna, bread, your favorite beverages, and any tabloid running a story on the latest Elvis sighting

The Date: Years after his death, Elvis Presley is still one of the most popular entertainers in the world. No entertainer has ever had or ever will have more charisma than "the king." All of us have a little bit of Elvis inside, and it is time that we be set free to express ourselves. Host an Elvis look-alike party. Encourage people to dress up like "the king." Sing or lip-synch to his songs and dine on peanut butter and bologna sandwiches. You can give out prizes for the best-dressed, worst-dressed, best singer, and worst singer. Take plenty of pictures, which can be used for blackmail purposes later!

44 Progressive Mock Kidnapping

The Essentials: A sense of adventure, a mode of transportation, willing friends, several free hours, and this book

The Date: Take no one against his or her will. To begin this date, visit a friend (whom you would like to date or are already dating) and ask that person to come along with you peacefully. After they have been "kidnapped," THEY choose the next person to "invite." That person then chooses, and so on. . . . Pick a specific number of people you hope to "acquire." Once you are all together, get out this book and choose a group date that you can enjoy together.

Twenty of the WORST Pick-up Lines Ever Uttered!

1. Just call me milk—I'll do your body good!
2. I want you almost as much as I want world peace.
3. You can forget about going to heaven because it's a sin to look that good.
4. How do you like me so far?
5. Do you believe in love at first sight, or do I need to walk by again?
6. We both know that I'm going to follow you home anyway, so why don't I just come along peacefully?
7. Do you know the difference between talking and sex? No? Then let's go up to my room and talk.
8. I didn't realize that angels flew so low.
9. Your father must have been a thief, because he stole all of ·the stars and put them in your eyes.
10. I envy your lipstick.
11. I just want to be loved—is that so wrong?
12. You remind me of a cold Pepsi—I've just gotta have it.
13. Do you believe in the hereafter? Good, then you know what I'm here after.
14. Your lips are like Lay's potato chips. You can't stop with just one.
15. If I had eleven roses and you, I'd have a dozen.
16. Hi, I'm new in town. Can I have directions to your place?
17. Didn't we bathe together as kids?
18. Baby, you look so sweet you're giving me a cavity.
19. Is it me or am I gorgeous?
20. I'd even marry your dog just to be related to you.

45 Partridge Family Party

The Essentials: A great sense of humor, all the Partridge Family albums, some reruns on tape or on television, snacks and beverages

The Date: Shirley, Keith, Lori, Danny, Chris, Tracey, and Mr. Kincaid. Even if we try, the reruns won't allow us to forget these characters! Admit it . . . you know the words to at least one Partridge Family song. Let's jog your memory. Finish this chorus: "Point me, in the direction of _____." This is a "groovy" group date. Encourage your friends to dress like their favorite cast member (featuring bell-bottoms, high boots, open

collars, or leisure suits). Count the number of times Keith shakes his hair, the number of times Danny is a tightwad, or the number of times someone says his name (he was a popular guy). Memories should come rushing back. For a special twist, rent a school bus as a limo for the evening.

(Answer to the quiz above: *Albuquerque*)

46 Antique Shopping

The Essentials: Relaxed attitude, time available for browsing, money for that "special purchase"

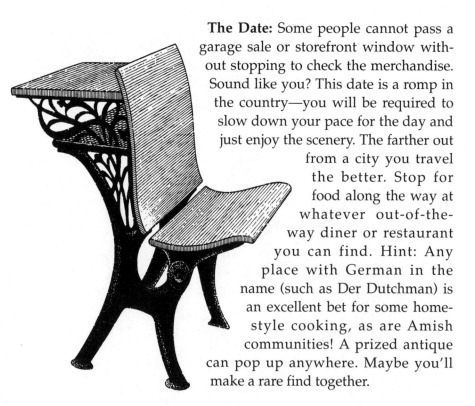

The Date: Some people cannot pass a garage sale or storefront window without stopping to check the merchandise. Sound like you? This date is a romp in the country—you will be required to slow down your pace for the day and just enjoy the scenery. The farther out from a city you travel the better. Stop for food along the way at whatever out-of-the-way diner or restaurant you can find. Hint: Any place with German in the name (such as Der Dutchman) is an excellent bet for some home-style cooking, as are Amish communities! A prized antique can pop up anywhere. Maybe you'll make a rare find together.

Flea Market or Garage Sale

The Essentials: Car, extra spending money, good walking shoes, good friends

The Date: Garage sales are great! Where else can you buy a good book for ten cents or a set of golf clubs for five dollars? One person's junk . . . . Remember, the price on every item is usually negotiable. Haggling is half the fun! The key to garage sale shopping is to get there early and snatch items up faster than the next guy! You and your date will discover a lot about each other's tastes as you browse through the bargains. Combine your cash, limit your spending, and go for it. You may be surprised at the "treasures" you discover.

48 Night Crawler Hunting and Fishing Competition

The Essentials: Two flashlights, two towels, two buckets partially filled with coffee grounds and dirt, a portable radio, very casual clothing, two fishing poles, a blanket, fishing licenses (possibly needed depending on where you fish), and a picnic lunch

The Date: First, you must catch the bait: night crawlers. Night crawlers come out after sunset. They are large earthworms that are difficult to catch because they are surprisingly fast when they feel threatened. You and your date set out, buckets and flashlights in hand, and begin to hunt night crawlers. To catch them, you must shine the light along the ground until you spot one. Then, quickly pin it against the ground with your towel, pick it up, and store it in the bucket of coffee grounds (while uttering such phrases as "you're fish food" and "come to Papa"). This activity will be more fun than you can imagine because of how hard they are to catch.

Next comes the fishing contest. The "catch" here is that you can use only the bait that you caught. Choose a nice, quiet, and secluded place to fish. This provides you with time to be alone and to get to know each other better. The winner is the person who catches the largest or most fish. What is the prize? The other person must clean and prepare the catch, or you can throw them all back in and eat the lunch you brought with you.

49 Twister Party

The Essentials: Good friends (dressed in solid colors to correspond to the Twister board colors: red, yellow, blue, and green), four or more Twister "boards," some taped funky music

The Date: You can picture this one: a large group of people resembling colorful crayons, twisted together like pretzels and laughing hysterically as "Play That Funky Music" pulses in the background. Yes, this is Twister madness! Think of a clever and severe penalty for anyone who loses his or her balance. The ultimate embarrassment would be to fall to the ground during the playing of any song from the *Saturday Night Fever* soundtrack. For an additional activity, incorporate a few hula hoops to loosen people up a bit. If a large number of people show up, feel free to combine several Twister boards into one mega people-scrambler!

50 College Campus Visit

The Essentials: Vehicle, road map, casual and comfortable clothing, college guide for the school you will visit (if available), tunes for the road

The Date: College campuses are often "miniature worlds of their own" tucked away in small towns and large cities all over the country. Often they are beautifully landscaped and bristling with activity and vitality. Escape together to a college campus nearby. Dine at a pub or eatery on campus. Take in a play or a concert. Work out in the recreation center. Spend time browsing through the library, bookstore, or chapel. Find a sunny, grassy area and relax. If one of you owns a dog, take it along to enjoy the new surroundings. College students will flock to animals because many miss their own pets. Prepare to meet many people this way.

51 Fantasy Vacation Without Leaving Home

The Essentials: An atlas, a videotape of an exotic destination, food from that country or region of the world, culturally appropriate regional music and decorations

The Date: From time to time we all dream of traveling to some exotic destination where we will be pampered and receive tender loving care. The fantasy vacation is one date that is great whether it becomes a romantic date for two or a group bonding time. Quite simply, you visit the library or any local travel agency and obtain a promotional videotape for an exotic destination. The Bahamas, Cancun, South America, Africa, the Swiss Alps, Europe, Hawaii, or Australia—the choice is up to your imagination. Decorate your place as if you were there, play music and serve a meal that would be reminiscent of that region. Make it seem, in as many aspects as possible, as if you are actually there. Research and attempt to imitate local customs, culture, and flavor. If you invite others, make sure that the invitation is festive. On the positive side, you won't experience jet lag and it should only cost you a fraction of what it would take to actually go there. The worst part is, you'll have to clean up after you're done and you may need to go to work the next day!

52 Sunrise Breakfast

The Essentials: Your favorite continental breakfast items, a few basic utensils, two blankets (one to sit on and one to cover in if it's a bit cool), and a camera

The Date: Enjoy the beginning of a new day by viewing one of the most spectacular moments in nature: the sunrise. Set your alarms, get up early, pack a light but delicious continental breakfast, and head to a romantic location in your area to catch the sunrise. Spread out one of the blankets and spend some quiet, very pleasant time together. Talk if you wish, snuggle, or just enjoy this wonder of nature. This is a super date if you have a busy day ahead and are unable to spend time together later.

53 The Godfather

The Essentials: A delicious pasta recipe, a hot loaf of Italian bread, olive oil, some traditional Italian music, pin-striped suits, and rented (or owned) videocassette copies of the *Godfather*, *Godfather II*, and *Godfather III* movies

The Date: This is a fine date for one couple or a group. To begin, dress up (both men and women) in pin-striped suits with white shirts and dark ties. Put on the Italian music (maybe the *Godfather* soundtrack) and sit down to a fine feast of pasta, garlic bread, meatballs, sausage, and salad. After dining, get comfortable and watch the *Godfather* trilogy. They are still among the finest films ever made, with megastars appearing in each one. Again, practice your "Italian" ("Youa talkin' toa mia Joey?"), and for amusement, count the total number of people killed (in one way or another) in all three films. Then, discuss the films, and each decide which one was your favorite and why.

71

1. Many songs, smells, and sights constantly remind you of that person.
2. There is a reprioritization of your life. Things that may have been very important in your life are quickly put in perspective in relation to that person.
3. You may experience a loss of appetite.
4. You may experience a loss of ability to concentrate (for any extended period).
5. You daydream about that person (or nightdream or both).
6. There may be a loss of ability to sleep well.
7. You think about that person many, many times a day, hour, or even minute.
8. You think about any future you may have with that person (mostly positive thoughts!).
9. You think about not being with that person in the future and how that will make you feel (and make the other person feel).
10. You experience an unusual feeling deep in the pit of your stomach. It might be fear. It might be joy. You can't be sure.
11. You experience complete selflessness. You can't do enough for that other person. You do your best to make sure that he/she is happy and that all needs are met.

Ways to Tell If You've Been Bitten by the Love Bug

12. You live for even the slightest contact with that person (a glance, a word, a touch, a smile). The other person means that much to you.
13. You read notes and letters over and over again that he or she wrote or sent you.
14. You love everything about the other person, even quirks (if he/she has any).
15. You think endlessly of things that you want to do with or for this person.
16. She or he is the last thing you think about before you go to sleep and the first thing you think about in the morning when you wake up.
17. You want to spend as much time as possible with this person.
18. You find yourself doodling the person's name. Some women may write their first name with his last to see if they like how it looks.
19. You hang on to articles of clothing that carry his or her smell (cologne or perfume).
20. You're very happy!

54 Parental / Grandparental Double Date

The Essentials: Patience

The Date: What more can you ask for? This date provides you with free entertainment (since most parents or grandparents are very amusing), and your parents or grandparents would be THRILLED that you actually wanted to spend time with them on a date. Be prepared to answer many questions about yourselves and the state of every aspect of your lives. But remember, it's still worth it! Your parents or grandparents might even volunteer to pick up the tab for the evening!

55 People-Watching

The Essentials: Tact, a great sense of humor, a prime location with plenty of foot traffic that affords you a comfortable place to relax

The Date: It might be a shopping mall or a park, a bowling alley or a carnival. Whichever location you choose, people-watching is a blast (and if you are in the right place, it's FREE!). People are unique in many ways from their body shape to their personality. Just sit back, relax, enjoy each other's company, and watch the world go by around you. Pay special attention to how much children look like their parents, how people resemble their pets, and how some people will display affection in public while others will not. Talk with your date about where you think each person, couple, or group may be headed or what they might be talking about. Imagine what you might ask each person if you had the chance.

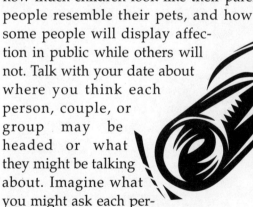

56 The Arcade

The Essentials: Spare change, transportation to the arcade, and a few free hours

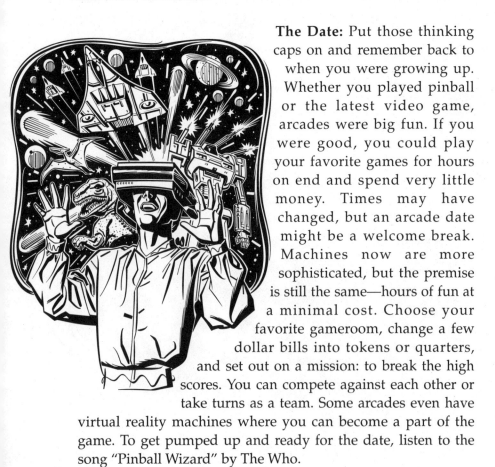

The Date: Put those thinking caps on and remember back to when you were growing up. Whether you played pinball or the latest video game, arcades were big fun. If you were good, you could play your favorite games for hours on end and spend very little money. Times may have changed, but an arcade date might be a welcome break. Machines now are more sophisticated, but the premise is still the same—hours of fun at a minimal cost. Choose your favorite gameroom, change a few dollar bills into tokens or quarters, and set out on a mission: to break the high scores. You can compete against each other or take turns as a team. Some arcades even have virtual reality machines where you can become a part of the game. To get pumped up and ready for the date, listen to the song "Pinball Wizard" by The Who.

57 A Different Las Vegas Weekend Getaway

The Essentials: An excellent travel agent, a few dollars saved up, comfortable shoes and clothing, and a free weekend

The Date: One of the fastest-growing cities in the United States is a perfect weekend getaway: Las Vegas. If you have a resourceful travel agent, this can be an inexpensive trip as well. Las Vegas is a city on the rise. It boasts several of the largest hotels in the world and seems to have something for everyone. There are theme parks, water sports, golf courses, glamorous shows, and great food at very reasonable prices. Under the lights at night, it is like no other city in the world. Hoover Dam and Lake Mead are a short trip away. You do not have to wager one cent. This could be a weekend you will never forget, and that's no gamble.

58 Blood Donation

The Essentials: A healthy supply of blood and a desire to donate

The Date: Many blood-banks nationwide are frequently in a crisis situation due to dwindling supplies of blood, and they can always use assistance. This date offers you the opportunity to be together and help out people you will probably never know. Your donation could save a life. How many dates will you go on where you can make that same claim? Donating blood won't take a lot of time or effort. Make sure that you give yourself time to recover before you go on another date described in this book. Giving blood would be a wonderful group activity. And you'll receive a treat before you leave.

Museum Adventure

The Essentials: A love of the arts (or at least a willingness to try!), comfortable clothing and shoes, transportation to and from the museum, and the proper entrance fee

The Date: Very few of us get exposed to as many cultural events as we should, and often, they are right at our fingertips. Many cities across the country offer cultural, educational, and enjoyable exhibits in any one of a number of museums. You might visit an art museum, natural history museum, or any one of our national Halls of Fame or military museums. You don't need to be an expert or critic; all it takes is a desire to learn and expose yourself to something new and different. This is a perfect date for a couple or a group. It could also lead to several dates if you attempt to visit a different museum each time.

60 Monday Night Football

The Essentials: A working television, your favorite snack foods and beverages, comfortable clothing and furniture, and a few close friends

The Date: With the arrival of Fall comes Monday Night Football. Love it or leave it, but at least try it with a different mind-set. Start preparing an hour before kickoff. Pop your favorite popcorn, prepare your favorite snacks, ice down your favorite beverages, and make the viewing area as comfortable as possible. Choose your favorite team and cheer them on. Have blankets and pillows available for any lulls in the action. Toss around a Nerf football or play a quick game of touch football during halftime or after the game. If you want to make things a bit more interesting, make a small non-monetary wager between couples (washing one another's car works well here!). This can lead to a date every Monday and is also a perfect group date.

61 Work Out Together

The Essentials: Proper exercise clothing and shoes

The Date: For many people, there is no better feeling than getting your heart pumping and your sweat rolling through exercise. You might go to a health club together, jog through each other's neighborhoods, do aerobics, or use a home gym. It doesn't matter how or where, it only matters that you *do* exercise. You can encourage each other as you exercise or simply tune in to the SOLOFLEX commercials for inspiration. The nice part about this date is that it can lead to many others and as you get into better condition, you'll both be around longer to share time in the future. Make sure to drink liquids to stay hydrated. After your workout, go out together for a healthy meal or snack.

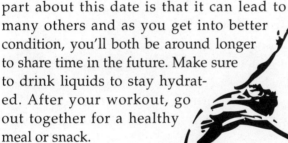

62 Plant a Garden

The Essentials: Old comfortable clothing, work gloves, a hose hooked up to a water source, a shovel and hard rake, various fruit and vegetable seeds or plants, a plot of land, and your favorite beverages

The Date: Here's one date that will definitely pay off in the future as long as you work as a team! Begin by marking off a plot of land (that you own or have permission to use!) and turning over the soil. If this gets tiresome, take turns. (If you are in no condition to shovel in the first place, rent a rototiller.) Then decide what you will plant. You might plant onions, tomatoes, broccoli, potatoes, lettuce, carrots, pumpkins, watermelons, corn, zucchini, or squash. What will you both love to eat once the garden is harvested? The beauty of this date is threefold:

1. Gardens need continuous care (which leads you to spend more time together).
2. You learn a lot about each other's determination in growing plants and taste in food.
3. In the end, there should be some tasty and healthy food for you both to enjoy!

63 Test-Drive a New Car

The Essentials: Transportation to get to the various car dealers you will visit, some money for "good faith" deposits, comfortable clothing and shoes, and a desire to be spontaneous!

The Date: The look, feel, and smell of a brand new car is irresistible. If you're in the market for a new automobile, then this date is a natural. If you're not in the market, it will still be fun, educational, and enjoyable. Start out the date by checking in the local newspapers for makes and models of cars that you would really like to see. Head to the appropriate dealerships. Be honest with them. If you're not in the market now (but will be in the future) tell them that you are trying to get a read on what your next car will be. Be prepared for most dealerships to want a "good faith deposit" (usually about $20) before they'll let you test drive a new car. Then, get behind that wheel and enjoy the ride. Be careful, and drive safely!

10 Important Things to Avoid on a First Date

#10 Sloppy food (such as chili, spaghetti, or anything you have to eat with your hands). You know darn well it will end up all over you!

#9 Talking about your ex-boyfriend or girlfriend. Never compare your date in any way to your ex-boyfriend or girlfriend.

#8 Bragging (over and over again about yourself and your accomplishments).

#7 Smelling like cigarette smoke. Bars are bad enough, you don't want to smell like one too. Avoid chewing tobacco as well.

#6 Ending long, awkward periods of uncomfortable silence by saying something really stupid. (Silence might not be so bad in comparison.)

#5   Calling your date by the wrong name. Make sure to never call him or her the name of your ex-boyfriend or girlfriend.

#4   Having a chunk of food stuck between your front teeth (that is assuming that you have front teeth).

#3   Extravagant dinners or long boring movies. The dinner will be expensive and expectations may surface. Opportunities are limited to communicate at a movie and sexually explicit scenes may cause embarrassment for both of you.

#2   Forgetting your wallet, purse, or money. No matter how hard you try to explain it, you will end up looking cheap and/or clueless.

#1   Being late (or not showing up at all!). You might as well stick a fork in yourself, because you're done!

64 Pamper Your Partner

The Essentials: Whatever your partner wants!

The Date: Every once in a while, it is a great feeling to be totally pampered, to have all of your needs met, without having to lift a finger or ask for special treatment. This date is designed with that premise in mind. Inform your date that for one day or evening or both, you will be pampering him or her. A few possible activities are: make a favorite meal (and then clean up), get freshly cut flowers, arrange a mini-shopping spree (with a spending limit), clean your date's home or apartment, do the laundry, arrange a professional massage, take the person to a favorite place or to see a favorite entertainer, band, show, or movie. Whatever will make your date optimally happy should be your goal.

65 Airport Rendezvous

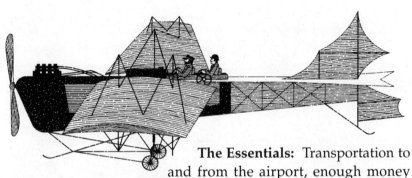

The Essentials: Transportation to and from the airport, enough money for lunch or dinner for two and parking, comfortable clothing and shoes

The Date: Airports are fast-paced, exciting places. People are always coming and going, and jets seem to take off almost every minute. This is a simple and interesting date. Drive to the nearest major airport. Park and go inside a terminal. Then, choose a lounge or restaurant in the terminal to have lunch or dinner (depending on what time it is). Most airports also have several great places to have dessert or take care of your sweet tooth. Take time to enjoy the people around you. You may see several reunions and a few separations. People in airports often run the gamut of emotions, and remember, people-watching is free. To have a thrill, stage a reunion between the two of you where one person pretends to have just unloaded and the other is anxiously awaiting the arrival. Embrace (and kiss?).

66 Sweet Tooth Satisfaction

The Essentials: A hunger for something sweet, a "sweetheart," a place that sells sweets

The Date: Remember the little malt shop around the corner where everyone went on hot summer nights for that special treat? Your mouth watered in anticipation of a soft-serve cone, a malt or milkshake, a root beer float, a cup of frozen yogurt, or a chocolate brownie. Sharing these moments and memories with that special someone can be satisfying and memorable. Buy one milkshake or root beer float to share with two straws—how romantic! Make it a tradition to meet at your favorite sweet spot at least once a month! Sit in the same booth each time and become a regular.

67 The Storefront Ride

The Essentials: A roll of quarters, transportation, and the urge to be spontaneous

The Date: Warning: you may want to invite a child on this date as some rides may be too small for adults! Rudolph the Red-Nosed Reindeer, a Bucking Bronco, a Carousel, "Flipper" the Dolphin: What do all of these have in common? You guessed it—they are all typical rides you can find if you travel around town looking in front of stores. This will certainly take some courage and craziness. Once on the ride, ham it up a bit by yelling, "Yee ha!" and swinging your arm in the air. You'll be amazed at how long that sucker goes on just one quarter when fifty people have gathered to watch. Remember to take turns!

68 A New Perspective

The Essentials: An open mind

The Date: It is often said that people are creatures of habit. We get comfortable doing things a certain way. It is difficult for us to alter our lifestyle or change our perspective. On this date, do just that. If you are right-handed, do as much as you can with your left hand. Blindfold each other and try to experience what it would be like to be blind (take turns acting as a guide for the other person). You may have to place a great deal of trust in others. Communicate without speaking a word. For an entire day, use mass transit (or a bike) if you normally take a car. Rearrange your house or apartment. Eat only one meal each day. Leave the television off for at least twenty-four hours. Be encouraged to attempt anything that would give you a new perspective on life or each other.

69 Driving Range / Miniature Golf

The Essentials: At least one set of golf clubs, transportation to the range and miniature golf course, enough money for a large bucket of golf balls, and two miniature golf passes

The Date: Golf can be a very fun sport but is one that demands a great deal of practice. Hopefully, the more you practice the more accurate and confident you will become. More practice means more time together. Find a local driving range facility and buy a bucket of practice balls to split between the two of you. If one of you already knows how to play, give the other a simple lesson. If neither of you knows how to play, consider taking a group lesson. Be very careful not to stand behind the other person as he or she swings as it could be highly dangerous. Try not to laugh at each other's shots. Be encouraging. After you are done at the range, travel to your favorite miniature golf course. The more windmills and clown mouths you have to go through, the better. Remember to take along some strong mosquito repellent!

70 Classic Board Games

The Essentials: Your favorite snack foods and beverages, comfortable clothing, and several of your favorite "classic" board games or favorite games from your childhood. Some suggested games are: Scrabble, Monopoly, Risk, Stratego, Battleship, Life, Clue, Operation, or good old checkers

The Date: Choose a night and a few of your favorite "classic" board games and let the fun begin. Put the names of up to ten board games (that you own) in a bowl and choose one. When you finish playing that game, choose another. Play as many as you have energy to complete. This would be a wonderful group dating opportunity as long as the people involved don't take the games too seriously. Remember, no matter who wins or loses, you've spent a great deal of time together and hopefully you've had some fun.

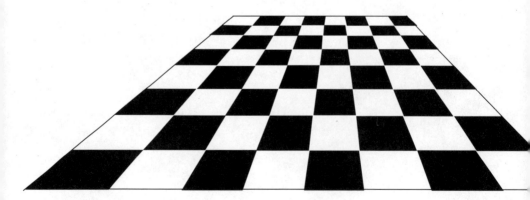

Bringing Back Romance!

Ways to Be More Thoughtful, Spontaneous, and Romantic

Suggestions for women from men . . .

* Try not to be sports "clueless." (Many men enjoy sports and want to talk about it with you.)
* Ask him out. Offer to drive. Make the arrangements. Pay for the date. He just shows up!
* Let him know that you appreciate his efforts and attention.
* Drop him a short note. Send him a flower or his favorite snack or food.
* Be prompt in responding to an offer for a date.
* Attempt something recreational even if you are not athletically inclined. Making an effort shows you're a sport.
* Don't compare him to, look at, or talk about other men when you're with him. (Men are highly jealous creatures.)
* Don't overreact when he wants to go "out with the guys."

Suggestions for men from women. . .

* Pay for the date with class. Don't make it a huge production.
* Drop her a note or write her a poem. It doesn't have to be long-winded, just heartfelt.
* Take her to places that she really enjoys and that make her happy.
* Don't look (gawk) at, or talk about other women when you are with her.

* Spend time alone with her. Focus on her. Listen to her. Take her away from her normal everyday routine and lifestyle. It doesn't have to be expensive, just a diversion.
* Make her a candlelight dinner that you prepare from scratch.
* Limit how much you talk (or brag) about sports.
* Open doors for her. Offer your coat when she might be cold. Don't let her walk immediately next to the curb.
* Take her shopping and don't complain!
* Make her a tape of some of your "special" songs from your times together.
* Avoid checking your watch as if there is a time limit on the date.

 # Show Off Your Hidden Talent

The Essentials: This will change for every dating couple depending on what talent each possesses

The Date: Each person has certain God-given abilities and talents. Often, however, the difficult part is getting a person to be open about his or her talents and to share them. You or your date might be a great singer or musician or athlete. Maybe one or both of you writes poetry or has a photographic memory. Maybe one or both of you can speak several languages. Sit down with your date and "interview" each other. Find out any hidden talents either of you might have and exhibit them for each other. Treat this not as a "show-off" date but as a get-to-know-each-other experience.

72 Learn to Rappel

The Essentials: The guts to rappel, a reliable facility with a qualified instructor, and enough money to cover the fee for two

The Date: When we are afraid to try new things, the solution is to take the risk out of the activity. In rappelling, the risk is, well—the potential of falling to the ground and splatting like a pancake! For this reason, you must make sure that you have chosen a reputable facility with a qualified staff that puts safety as their first priority. Rappelling is one of the most exciting activities you can undertake where YOU control the rate of speed at which you travel. The date would consist of professional instruction on rappelling and the belay position (the person on the ground holding the ends of the rope for emergency safety purposes) and then the opportunity to try it yourself. If you are scared of heights, this is a perfect activity to get over that fear. Rappelling will also offer you both the opportunity to support each other through a difficult and challenging activity. This could be a super group date as well.

73 TV Shopping Channel

The Essentials: A phone, cable TV that carries shopping channels, and money to spend

The Date: If you are determined to stay home and watch TV, why not add a little spunk to the evening by having a Shopping Channel Date. Flip to any shopping channel and get the feel for how it operates (you may even call the 1-800 number on the screen to ask specific questions). Notice how the price sometimes gets lower as the time limit runs out (last minute incentive!). Actually make a purchase that you both could use or enjoy (a cooler, an autographed baseball, stereo headphones, matching his/her slippers). Hurry! You may miss out on a good deal! Be careful, you might just get hooked on television shopping. This idea may also work for a group.

74 Two Is More Fun Than One!

The Essentials: Creative imaginations

The Date: This dating idea is actually a series of activities to be enjoyed by couples. Some suggested activities are:

* Wash, cut, and style each other's hair
* Put together a jigsaw puzzle
* Fly a kite at a park or field
* Ride a bicycle built for two
* Water-ski
* Take a self-defense class
* Pull each other in an old red wagon
* Watch Jeopardy and compete
* Take turns giving each other backrubs
* Build a snowman
* Bombard each other with water balloons

Remember, the goal is to spend enjoyable, affordable time together. Done properly, this idea could lead to several dates!

February 1-14 Progressive Date

The Essentials: A creative imagination and about $40

The Date: Valentine's Day—how quickly it sneaks up on us! No matter how good our intentions, most of us wait until the last minute and then opt for the old standby of high-priced roses and fattening (yet delicious) candy. Here is a way to turn this holiday into a fun and progressive dating experience. From February 1 through 13, present your partner with a small gift accom-

panied by a single piece to a puzzle (that you designed). You don't need to spend a great deal on these gifts. The fact that you have been thoughtful and creative enough to get one for each day means more than any expensive present. Then, on February 14, give your partner the culminating gift (it should be the nicest gift) and the final piece to the puzzle. Make sure that the puzzle's message is kept a secret until the final piece is in place.

76 Flapjack Madness

The Essentials: Pancake mix, fresh fruit, several types of pancake syrup, and cold milk

The Date: When you're hungry for pancakes—nothing else will do. Make it breakfast for two or invite several friends over and ask each one to bring a different fruit or type of syrup. You supply the meeting place (complete with kitchen), the pancake mix, the ice cold milk, and the morning paper. Then start flipping flapjacks! People can take turns preparing their favorite cakes, or several of you can cook to order for everyone else. If you arrange to have this date in the morning, it leaves time later in the day to try out another dating idea from this book. Bon appetit!

77 Just Like Child's Play

The Essentials: A jump rope, marbles, jacks, Cracker Jacks, a kickball, bubbles and bubble blower, bubble gum, and jelly beans

The Date: This date will allow you and your young-at-heart partner to return to those carefree days of youth when your only work was called *play*. Acquire some jacks, a jump rope, marbles, bubbles, a kickball, bubble gum, and Cracker Jacks. Head to the nearest grade school playground. Spend a few hours trying out each of the games you brought with you, then branch off to the swings, the monkey bars, tetherball, or the kickball diamond. For a few hours, rid your minds of any worries you may have and simply enjoy each other's company. This also could be a splendid group date for spontaneous and good-natured people.

78 | Where Were You When It Happened?

The Essentials: A pad of paper and pencil for every person involved, comfortable clothing and surroundings, your favorite snacks and beverages, and an hourglass

The Date: Certain happenings or events in American (and world) history have made such a lasting impact on people that at the mere mention of the topic they can immediately recall where they were, what they were doing, what they were feeling, and how they reacted. The memories are as vivid to them today as if it happened just five minutes ago. Whether it be the assassination of John F. Kennedy, Robert F. Kennedy, Martin Luther King, Jr.; the first person walking on the moon; or the Space Shuttle disaster, it is uncanny how quickly we recall our feelings.

Have participants take a few minutes and make a list of some of the major events they recall from history. Encourage each person to compile a list with both positive and negative historical events and then place each idea on a slip of paper. Collect all the slips and place them in a container. All involved can then take turns pulling out an "event" and talking about what it meant (and still means) to them. When each person begins, start the hourglass. When it is done, so is the speaker. Then others can provide their feelings as well. This could turn out to be a wonderful time of sharing and getting to know one another better.

Kiss-off Quotes

Quotes used to end a relationship

1. "We're getting too serious too quickly."

2. "Let's see other people for awhile and determine whether we are right for each other."

3. "I need some time." "I need some space."

4. "You're the right person at the wrong time in my life."

5. "My 'ex' and I have decided to give it another try."

6. "I really just want to be friends."

7. "This will hurt me a lot more than it will hurt you."

8. "You're like a brother (or sister) to me!" "You remind me of my mother (or father)."

9. "You're the type of person I would marry some day, but not date right now!"

10. "I love you, but I'm not *in* love with you!"

79 Reliving Your First Date

The Essentials: The essentials will be different for each couple, depending on where the first date occurred

The Date: Remember back to your first date? It probably went something like this: butterflies in your stomach, sweaty palms, unsure of what to say or how to act, wanting to make sure your date had a great time. On this date, reenact all the special moments of your first date together. Return to the same location. Order the same food. Make the same mistakes. Forget your money—again! Not only will it be fun to reminisce, but both of you will observe just how far your relationship has matured.

80 Video Interview

The Essentials: A working video camera, a list of questions you would like to ask your dating partner

The Date: This is an experience to treasure for a lifetime (or for as long as the videotape exists). Set up a comfortable, well-lit area and conduct personal, one-on-one interviews with each other. Have some questions prepared, but feel free to be spontaneous. Let the conversation head in any direction. Some possible questions:

* What is your fondest childhood memory?

* What qualities do you admire in men (or women)?

* If you could change places with any person in history, who would it be? Why?

* What is the one achievement in your life of which you are most proud?

* What are your top five favorite movies? Actors? Actresses? Books?

* What really bothers you, and how do you handle it?

The possibilities are endless, and you'll discover a lot about each other. This may take more than one date, depending upon how verbal you are.

81 A Dollar or Less

The Essentials: $10.00 each, and a store that sells items at $1.00 or less

The Date: Attention shoppers! Dollar stores are popping up all over the country. How can you turn this into a dating and shopping extravaganza? Easily! Together, go to one of those stores, each armed with $10.00 to spend on the other. Shop separately and keep what you buy a surprise. When you get home, wrap up each gift individually. Then, one at a time (and alternating between you), open each gift. This should be loads of fun, and each of you will end up with at least ten new items.

82

Up, Up, and Away!

The Essentials: A hot-air balloon-ride facility, qualified training and operating staff, a light continental breakfast or picnic lunch or dinner for three, enough money for a ride for two, and a camera

The Date: Take advantage of a spectacular sunrise, warm afternoon, or gorgeous evening by enjoying it high in the sky on a hot-air balloon ride. Hot-air balloon facilities can be found all over the country and are relatively affordable, considering the excitement they offer. Do some research and choose a reputable location with a qualified staff. Pack a light breakfast, lunch, or dinner for three (remember the balloon operator), and head up into the sky. The views should be breathtaking and the date unique. Take some pictures to capture the moment on film.

When an Extended

When a long-term relationship ends, there is a sense of personal loss between those involved. No longer will they see each other on a regular basis, nor will they share those special times, places, moments, intimate secrets or conversations. Songs, smells, television shows, places, foods, and so many things make us continue to think about the other person. It is hard to let the relationship end. It is possible that when our ex-partners leave us, they know as much or more about our beliefs, habits, and lifestyles as any member of our family or our closest personal friend. The thought of our ex-partner having the same experiences with another person can be very distressing. It is not unusual to feel violated. Following a tough breakup, we may want to avoid people or another relationship for a long time. The following suggestions might help to relieve some of the pain involved:

1. Don't leave town. The same things that remind you of the person locally will exist in other locations as well.

2. Don't rush out and attempt to date someone on the rebound immediately following the breakup. You might have the tendency to compare that person to your ex-partner.

3. Don't burn your bridges. Be careful of the things you say and do. Avoid malicious behavior directed toward your ex-partner (especially as a way of making yourself feel better). You never know when the candle may burn brightly again. Many things are better left unsaid.

4. Take good care of yourself. Eat healthy foods, read for pleasure, stay current, work out. This will catch the attention of

Relationship Ends

others and build up your confidence and self-esteem. Always be prepared for a new relationship to develop, but be patient!

5. Turn to your close friends for support and social life. Avoid seeking pity from them, but rely on their solid friendship and the opportunity to meet others. Tell them how you are feeling and then move on—start to put your social life back together. Remember, every day you are feeling sorry for yourself or living in the past, is a day that you are not living life to its fullest or working on enhancing it.

6. Break your normal routines. Try some different foods, visit new locations, read an exciting novel, watch different shows, or take a different route to work.

7. Don't diet. When you fall off the dietary wagon (and you will), you'll feel twice as bad about yourself and your lack of self-control. It is hard enough to diet under normal circumstances.

8. Dress up and go shopping. At least window shop, if you don't have any extra funds available. Malls can be a great place to meet new people. Smile! It is tremendously difficult to be depressed when you are smiling.

9. Join a social or civic group. It could be a church group, health club, or a community activity. Just being around others who are planning or working on something positive can give you a big lift.

10. Volunteer at a nursing home, soup kitchen, pet shelter, children's hospital, or hospice. Helping out those less fortunate will put your own situation in perspective.

83 Dancing Lessons

The Essentials: Comfortable clothing and shoes, a desire to learn, an open mind, and a great instructor

The Date: Dancing, for many, is a lost art. Yet it can be one of the most enjoyable activities on a date. This date will provide you with time to spend together while learning something new. Choose a style  that both of you would like to learn: swing dancing, line dancing, tap dancing, Lambada, square dancing, ballroom dancing, or even clogging! Research and choose a reputable dance studio and begin your lessons, or rent an instructional video. Don't worry about being uncoordinated at the beginning. Enjoy the experience and support each other—literally. Once you have learned several different dance steps, you'll want to go out on the town and show off some of your moves.

84 Corn and Fish Roast

The Essentials: Fresh corn on the cob (still in the husk), milk, butter or margarine, your favorite fresh fish, plates and eating utensils, a shovel, self-lighting charcoal, and aluminum foil

The Date: Get ready for a feast! First, you need to handpick or purchase several ears of fresh corn on the cob. Leave them in their husks. Soak the ears at least two or three hours in fresh milk. Keep the milk fairly cold, so that it doesn't spoil or turn. While the corn is soaking, filet your fresh fish (if this has not already been done for you). Place the fish inside foil, with a few pats of butter or margarine and your favorite spices. Fold the foil package up tightly and keep it cool until you're ready to cook. Next, you must dig a small pit in the ground. It need be only large enough to handle the charcoal and food you'll be placing inside. Fill the hole half full of charcoal and ignite it. When the coals have turned a bright red, place the corn (wrapped in foil) and the fish on top, and then cover it up with the dirt you displaced when forming the hole. In 45 minutes to an hour, you should have a feast you'll long remember. Invite others for a real party!

85 BYOF Cookout

The Essentials: A good barbecue grill, cooking utensils, your favorite music and beverages

The Date: The problem with cookouts is that too often, one person or family must supply food for the entire outing. This can be expensive and time consuming. This date removes all the worry so that people can eat and have a good time. Host a barbecue party with a twist. Inform others that you will supply the grill, beverages, plates, utensils, and marshmallows. The rest of the party will be BYOF (Bring Your Own Food). If all agree, they can bring a bit more than they need for themselves and share it. This will provide a smorgasbord feast for all. For entertainment, bring along a set of horseshoes, badminton, or volleyball setup, a slip and slide, or a Frisbee and hacky sack.

T-Shirt Graffiti Party

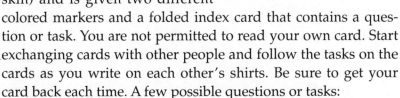

The Essentials: Two white undershirts per person, several non-permanent markers, index cards, and a fun-loving attitude

The Date: Don't take it personally, but at the conclusion of this date, people will be able to read you like a book. This is a group date that goes like this—each person wears two white T-shirts (one on top of the other so that the markers don't bleed through onto the skin) and is given two different colored markers and a folded index card that contains a question or task. You are not permitted to read your own card. Start exchanging cards with other people and follow the tasks on the cards as you write on each other's shirts. Be sure to get your card back each time. A few possible questions or tasks:

* Draw the animal that most resembles me.
* Draw three words that best describe me.
* What famous person do I remind you of?

At the end of the evening, you finally get to read your card and your shirt, and then attempt to find out who drew what!

14 Ways to Rekindle Romance This Valentine's Day

1. Make your significant other a card, instead of buying one from a store. No matter how bad an artist you are, it is the thought that counts!

2. Arrange for your friends to dress up as waiters and waitresses to serve you and your partner a romantic, secluded candlelight dinner!

3. Give your partner a small gift each day, from February 1 through February 13. Accompany each gift with a word or sentence—part of a message. The last gift on February 14 should be a special gift and contain the conclusion of the message.

4. Tell your partner to dress nicely. Say that you are going out for a special dinner. Take real plates, napkins, silverware, candles, and glasses, and go have dinner at a fast-food restaurant.

5. Send your partner a single flower, along with a short but sweet message from you. It doesn't need to be a rose, but if you decide to send one, make it a color other than red. Be different! Be romantic!

6. Send your partner on a February-14 scavenger hunt that ultimately brings him/her back to you at a romantic destination or somewhere that sparks fond memories.

7. Do something against your nature. Whether it be a play, a visit to the zoo, a park, a museum, ice skating, roller skating, or attending a sports event, choose an event or activity to show that you are able to try something new, from time to time!

8. Offer your partner a chance to make three wishes, which you will do your best to make come true (if they are realistic and within your limits!).

9. Arrange for your partner to go to a professional health spa, including a massage, steam, sauna, and so on.

10. Take your partner on a progressive meal date. Have an appetizer at one restaurant, your main course at a second, and dessert at a third (or at a special place you both enjoy).

11. Throw a party and invite 14 of your closest friends (or 14 couples, if you are married). Ask each person or couple to bring a different food, so that you will have 14 different delicacies. A spin-off would be for you and your partner to spend the day making ice cream. Invite 14 friends or couples, and ask each to bring a different topping (bananas, nuts, various fruit toppings, chocolate, whipped cream, etc.).

12. Volunteer with your partner.

   * Visit a nursing home and give small cards and sweets to those who may not receive a visitor that day. The joy you give to others will make you feel better about yourselves and each other.

   * A second idea: go out and buy 14 food items and take them to a local food bank or soup kitchen. You may even want to volunteer to work that day.

   * Visit a pet shelter and play with the animals. You'd be surprised what a little love will do for them.

13. Spend the day visiting your past. Look at your old high school yearbooks and read what people said about you, listen to music from 5, 10, 15 years ago, watch an Elvis movie, go to an arcade, fly a kite, or ride a bike built for two.

14. Do absolutely nothing! Build a roaring fire (in a fireplace!), make hot cocoa, smores, and just snuggle!

87 Save It, Wrap It, Spend It!

The Essentials: All your loose change, coin wrappers, and this book!

The Date: Loose change can be found just about anywhere: beneath seat cushions, under the couch, at the bottom and the back of drawers, in the depths of your purse, on the floor of your car, in your pockets. The hiding locations are too numerous to mention. Beginning today, make a pact with your dating partner that for the next several months, both of you will save *all* the change you find. At the end of that time, you will combine all your change into one pile and wrap it all up. Then you can choose one or several ideas from this book and use that "extra" money to have a great time.

88 Dress-Like-the-Host Party

The Essentials: A sense of humor, appropriate clothing, your favorite snack foods and beverages, and some good music

The Date: Each of us has a distinctive style that is all our own. This is a group date that calls for a keen sense of humor on behalf of the host. The host may not even know that he or she is the focus of the party until it is too late. When one of your friends is having a party, get together with other friends to dress like the host. It is important that they all know the host very well so that they can dress the part. Have prizes ready for the person who looks most like the host or who best captures the host's style. It is best if the "butt" of this party acts as the judge (who better to judge?). All decisions are final!

89 Country Western Night

The Essentials: A pair of jeans, a country-style shirt, a cowboy hat, cowboy boots, and an open mind

The Date: Country music is sweeping the nation. It is No. 1 in several of the larger radio markets in the United States. Many country-western establishments are opening up as well, so it is time to take advantage of this golden opportunity. Get all "dudded up" (i.e., looking good) in your best country outfit and head out for a night on the town. Choose a location that has a live band, mechanical bull riding, and line-dancing lessons. Some places may even have karaoke at your disposal, so that you can show off those hidden talents. If you really want to get yourself in the mood before you go, rent and watch the movie *Urban Cowboy*, starring John Travolta. But don't let it scare you off the date!

 90 Baking Cookies

The Essentials: All the essential ingredients needed to make your favorite cookies

The Date: Moist, warm, delicious cookies. With ice-cold milk, there is nothing on earth to compare. But how many of us really know how to make great cookies? This date will provide three very positive things: (1) you will spend time with your dating partner; (2) you will be forced to work as a team; (3) at the end, you should have several dozen cookies to consume or share (or both). As a team, decide on the type of cookies you'll attempt to prepare, then divide the tasks evenly. You may want to have some of your favorite music playing in the background, but not too loud. You need to be able to communicate and hear the directions. After you finish cooking, pour two glasses of cold milk, and enjoy the fruits of your labor. If you made more cookies than you need, share them!

91 The Bus Loop

The Essentials: Enough time and money to ride the complete bus loop of your city, or a city near you

The Date: In our fast-paced world, we don't take time to notice the individuals and neighborhoods around us. This date is the perfect opportunity to hang out with many different and diverse groups of people, as you cruise around town on a bus. You may feel inclined to get off and take in some scenes along the way, or just have a conversation with people in particular neighborhoods. We can live in a city our entire lives and never leave our personal safety zone. This is your chance to experience, firsthand, what your city has to offer. Eat, shop, or relax in the different areas of your city.

92 Tie-Dye Mania

The Essentials: Dye, T-shirt, rubber bands, old tub for dye, creative ideas for designs, and some oldies music

The Date: We all need a creative release. When we finger-painted in kindergarten or made sand castles at the beach, we were in our element, doing what came naturally. As an older or younger adult, we still have the urge to create, but we lack the opportunity. Get that carefree feeling again by creating a tie-dyed T-shirt. Set up bowls of varying dye colors, pinch off sections of your T-shirt with rubber bands, dip them in, and let them dry. What comes out of this process will be your own creation and will save you money over store-bought apparel. To add to the ambiance of the date, play some mem-ory-raising 60s music in the background. The *Beatles White Album* or the soundtrack to *The Big Chill* would do nicely.

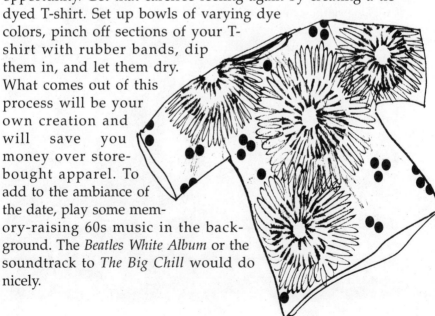

93 Toy Store Shopping

The Essentials: Transportation, coupons, checkbook or money

The Date: Visit a mega toy store and, for once, shop for yourselves. You will be amazed at the huge selection of toys available today. From colored Gak to bubble blowers and everything imaginable, this is the perfect date to regress to childhood and indulge yourself. Walk the aisles together, try out some of the demonstration models, then purchase a few of your favorite items, head home, and begin to play. Put yourselves on a spending limit and stick to it. Once you start browsing through the store, you'll probably see many things that grab your interest. Exercise self-control—toys today aren't always inexpensive. This date should lead to hours of laughter and storytelling about your childhood and your childhood pastimes.

How to Have a Successful Blind Date

- Gauge how much you trust the judgment of the person who has made the arrangements for you! Base your decision on how much you trust this person and how much you desire to meet someone new.

- Find out as much as you can about the person you'll be going out with. However, be careful not to regurgitate everything you have learned or you'll look like a detective.

- If there will be expenses during the date, discuss who will pay right away.

- Don't hold unrealistic expectations about the person you will meet or the success of the date. We all seem to hold a picture of the person we expect to show up, and then when the person arrives we are either disappointed or elated. Additionally, getting out is a positive experience in itself.

- If you're a little bit nervous, talk about it with the other person. Chances are, he or she is as anxious as you, and it will ease the situation.

- Go into the date expecting to have an enjoyable time. Often people enter a blind date with the expectation that they will not enjoy themselves or their company.

- Have up to five options ready on how you will suggest that you spend your time together. Be prepared for the person just to want to "hang out" or do something extremely casual. Be flexible and versatile.

- Try to choose an activity that becomes the focal point of the date: a circus, bowling, an arcade, a play—anything active that eases the stress on the two of you.

- Bring your date a flower or a small gift (inexpensive) to express welcome.

- Avoid alcohol. The last thing you want to do on a first date is to lose control and not remember it in the morning.

94 Bathing Rover

The Essentials: Flea shampoo, warm tub of water, old towels, brush, and patience

The Date: Most dogs enjoy a warm, leisurely bath. Others, however, find the idea downright scary. First, as the loving dating couple that you are, come to an agreement that neither of you will "bail out" on the other when the going gets tough! Wet the dog down (with warm water), then lather it up with special flea shampoo (try not to use "people shampoo" as this tends to dry out the dog's skin). Leave the shampoo on for several minutes so any vermin will be killed. Next, rinse the dog and towel dry. Stand back and watch as the dog shakes water in all directions! If your dog will sit still, do a "pawdicure" with special dog nail clippers (be sure not to cut too short). Finally, finish off the adventure by brushing out the dog's coat. Reward yourselves with a refreshing beverage of your choice. Prepare to laugh nonstop.

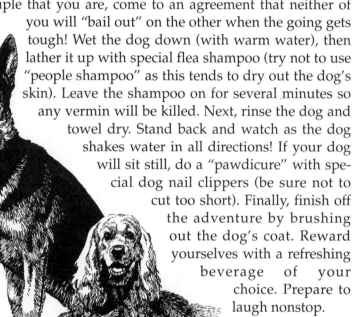

95 Aquarium Warming Party

The Essentials: An aquarium, a few fish, and several very spontaneous friends

The Date: Remember when you won those goldfish at the carnival ring-toss game? You brought them home and had no idea where to put them or how to take care of them. It has been observed that watching fish swim in an aquarium can reduce people's blood pressure and help them relax. So throw a party together that may help extend your lives. Invite people over and ask each one to bring an inexpensive fixture that would be found in an average aquarium. It might be a fake rock or shipwreck, a mermaid or treasure chest. What they bring does not matter. (You didn't have any items before the party, did you?) To add to the mood of the event, watch any of the following movies: *Jaws, Jaws II, Jaws III,* or *The Incredible Mr. Limpet.* For nourishment, serve goldfish crackers or cookies.

96 Fireplace Embrace

The Essentials: Roasting fire, smores ingredients, favorite tunes, poetry, soft rug or blankets, and pillows

The Date: What could be more romantic than snuggling by a fire with your loved one? Feel free to roast popcorn over the fire or create smores (chocolate and marshmallows melted between two graham crackers). Softly play selections from your favorite musicians, read poetry to each other, or just talk. The focus here is spending uninterrupted time together and getting to know each other better. If you wish, watch a romantic movie together as well. A few suggestions are: *When Harry Met Sally, Sleepless in Seattle, Far and Away,* or *Ghost.* Suggested movies to avoid: *Fatal Attraction, Final Analysis,* or *Basic Instinct.*

97 Batting Cage

The Essentials: Your favorite wood or aluminum bat, an approved batting helmet, batting glove, and quarters for the cage

The Date: Some major league baseball players make hitting look so easy. Amazingly, they follow a small round ball (approaching at speeds of over 100 miles per hour in some cases), make contact with a curved bat, and manage to hit it squarely. How is this done? Practice. Set out as a couple with equipment and quarters in hand and find a well-run local batting cage. Get all of your gear ready, feed the machine, then step in and take your cuts. If the fast-pitch baseball machine is too intense, most cages also have slower softball cages available. Batting gloves may help you to keep a better grip on the bat. Encourage each other and keep track of how well you do. The next day, get together for back and shoulder rubs.

Bathrobe and Boxers Party

The Essentials: Outrageous boxer shorts, a comfortable bathrobe, good music, and your favorite snacks and beverages

The Date: Brace yourself for continuous fun and laughter. Together, throw a party and invite your friends. State on the invitation that, to enter, they must be wearing only a top (of their choice) boxer shorts, and a bathrobe. If you don't already own a hot tub or spa, rent one for the evening. If you do this, encourage people to bring a towel and a change of clothing. For added ambiance, have the movie *Splash* playing in the background. To set the "morning mood," serve breakfast foods as a snack and decorate with rolled-up newspapers. Guys can even go unshaven to this party! You may want to sponsor a sexiest (or least sexy) legs contest (for men and women) as well as the most outrageous boxer shorts award.

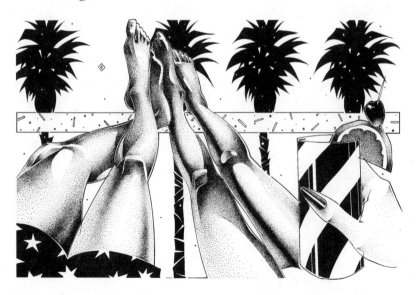

Ten Helpful Hints on Effective Dating Communication

1. ASK OPEN-ENDED QUESTIONS. Allow your dating partner (or spouse) to talk about himself or herself. People are often eager to talk about themselves and are pleased that you have shown an interest. Plus, it is a topic they are familiar with and will feel comfortable discussing.

2. LISTEN INTENTLY. *Do not* spend the time thinking about and planning what your response will be! Men are usually quick to talk about themselves but have difficulty listening effectively. Women are often hesitant to disclose personal information but are intense listeners.

3. FIND A COMMON DENOMINATOR. Keep trying until you find a subject that is interesting to both of you. You might be surprised how much you actually have in common.

4. AVOID MOVIES OR EXTRAVAGANT DINNERS AS FIRST DATES. Both of these options offer little chance for creative conversation and may lead to embarrassing moments of silence or awkwardness (such as during a movie when highly seductive, suggestive, or sexually explicit scenes appear), forced conversation, or questionable etiquette (during dinner, did I use the correct fork and spoon?).

5. BE KNOWLEDGEABLE AND ARTICULATE. Be able to talk about what is happening in the world around you (locally, regionally, and nationally). Men, avoid over-discussing the latest on sports television!

**6. BE CAREFUL NOT TO CONVEY THE WRONG MES-
SAGE.** An accidental or inappropriate verbal or nonverbal ges-
ture or comment could lead to a misperceived cue. If you feel
you may have given your date the wrong idea, be honest
immediately and rectify the situation before it gets blown out
of proportion.

**7. ATTEMPT SOME HUMOR, BUT IF YOU'RE FAILING,
CHILL OUT!** A good sense of humor, when timely and appropriate, can really loosen people up. Conversely, misplaced or
sad attempts at being funny can lead to embarrassing and irre-
versible failures. Avoid being "funny" all the time. It can get
old very fast!

**8. ALLOW THE DATE TO BE THE FOCAL POINT FOR
CONVERSATION.** Mutually select a fun, entertaining, interesting, and spontaneous date that will provide a good opportunity for conversation to develop. Maybe a circus, people-
watching, a picnic, riding a bike built for two, professional
wrestling, making ice cream, etc.

9. JUST BE YOURSELF. If you try and pretend to be "someone else," sooner or later you will revert back to who you really
are and your date will wonder, "Who is this person—person A
or person B?"

10. BE POLITE, CARING, AND THOUGHTFUL. Remember
what your date likes and dislikes. Make choices based on the
information he or she provides for you. Go the extra mile when
a situation presents itself. Set yourself apart from the rest!

99 Breakfast on the Range

The Essentials: Water in a jug, breakfast foods (omelet ingredients), campfire and cooking tools, firewood and starter wood, "hobo pie" iron

The Date: This date will require some planning, but the results are incredible! To start, travel by horseback to a secluded country location. Stop for a campfire-style country breakfast complete with omelets, hobo pies (two slices of bread with filling of your choice: jam, cheese/jalapeño peppers, meat), orange juice, and sausage. Watching the sunrise can be breathtaking, especially if you are with someone you care for. If there is a guide with you, bring enough food along to feed three. You'll enjoy the trip out to the breakfast site and the trip back to the stables. Ask the guide for a few horses with "spunk." Use water to make sure fire is completely extinguished.

100 Talk Radio Call-in

The Essentials: A radio, a telephone, and an opinion

The Date: Each of us has, at some point, listened to a talk-radio program. Sometimes we agree with the opinions we hear. Other times we disagree. We may even feel moved enough to want to respond with our own opinion. This date will allow you to give your personal input (as a team if you wish). Get comfortable with your dating partner and tune in to a talk-radio program. Listen for a while and, at an appropriate moment, call in! It will be exciting to be a part of the action, and you will probably encourage someone else to call to respond to your comments. If you have trouble getting through with your "two cents," turn to date number 28 and write an editorial for your local paper!

101 Paint by Number

The Essentials: Special paint-by-number kit and two brushes

The Date: Have you ever uttered the quote, "I'm such a bad artist I can't even draw stick figures!" Well, even if you are not a great artist, you will thoroughly enjoy this creative date! All you have to be able to do is count. Select a picture that best represents your feelings for your date. It could be a beautiful sunset, a race car going around a turn, or a waterfall. Whatever the scene, spend time together while painting by numbers. You will probably be very surprised by your results. For refreshments, indulge in cookies and milk or fruit drink.

36856126547
404782067470
0356806543
7568986554
907458
4569
7887
8967
845
56
75
6
7

102 Create Your Own Date!

The Essentials:

The Date:

Brainstorm List of Creative Dating Ideas

Athletic/"Active" Dates:

Go camping
Go ice skating or roller skating
Go moped riding
Go horseback riding
Play Frisbee
Play hacky-sack
Go fishing
Play tennis
Go to the driving range
Go miniature golfing
Play volleyball
Play wallyball
Go whitewater rafting
Hot-air balloon ride
Play football in the rain or mud
Go dancing
Ride a bike built for 2
Take a helicopter ride
Rake leaves in a pile & jump in
Go waterskiing
Play racquetball
Play handball
Go sailing
Go deep-sea fishing
Windsurf
Parasail
Parachute
Hang-glide
Take flying lessons together
Jet ski

Climb trees together
Go to a playground together
Wash each other's cars
Take a riverboat cruise
Go to the horse races
Go sled riding
Play broomball
Take pictures of the season
Work out together
Take aerobics together
Go to an amusement park
Build a snowman/make angels
Ride a ferry or steamboat
Play Photon/Laser Tag
Sunbathe
Waterslide
Learn to rock climb
Learn to rappel
Go swimming
Go bowling
Run together in the rain
Visit a city park
Cook out
Play badminton
Play croquet
Play 1-on-1 basketball
Scuba dive
Learn to kayak
Visit caves
Ride go-carts

Walk your dog
Take self-defense courses
Play beach volleyball
Play hide and seek
Fly a kite at a park or field

Catch fireflies
Play a game of bocce ball
Take turns giving backrubs
Have a snowball fight

Social or Group Dates:

Walk through a zoo
Go to a mall and shop
Go to a mall and just watch
  people
See a play
Have a small party
Play board games
Coach a little kids team
Go to a boating show together
Go to an airshow
Visit each other's grandparents
Adopt a grandparent
Adopt a little brother or sister
Go to a drive-in
Go to church together
Go to a car show
Take a hobby class together
Make your own video
Go to an all-u-can eat buffet
Go to a movie

Visit friends
Fast food restaurant hopping
Go watch big-time wrestling
Go to a ballet or creative dance
Go to an ice-skating show
Attend a circus
Attend university-sponsored
  events
Have a progressive dinner
Visit other colleges
Go out for coffee/doughnuts
Visit a haunted house
Go see fireworks
Visit rummage sales
Visit flea markets
Visit garage sales
Hayride
Cruise in a convertible
Progressive mock-kidnap party

Quiet Dates:

Go for a country drive
Go for a sunset walk
Go for a moonlight walk
Go stargazing
Cook dinner for each other

Watch TV together
Rent movies and a VCR
Take a carriage ride
Study together
Have a picnic in your room

Look at each other's baby pix
Feed ducks at a lake or pond
Look at Christmas lights
Decorate your Christmas tree
Just hang out together
Go to a museum
Go to an art gallery
Get up early and watch the
    sunrise
Watch the sunset
Graveyard walk (daylight)
Just plain snuggle
Bake cookies together
Put together a puzzle
Build models

Do laundry together
Make caramel/candy apples
Carve a jack-o'-lantern together
Make ice cream
Read old high school yearbooks
Play cards
White rose petal scavenger hunt
Celebrate Elvis's birthday
Picnic on 50 yard line, half
    court, pitcher's mound, 18th
    green
Progressive restaurant eating
    (Names A to Z)

Musical or Educational Dates:

See a musical
Go to an opera
Listen to grandparents' stories
Go to a concert
Go to the symphony or pops
    Listen to records, tapes, or
    CDs
Read the Bible
Visit another city

Go to SeaWorld or a similar place
Go out for a cultural dinner
Study together
Go to a bookstore together
Visit a children's hospital
Go hear jazz or reggae
Take a Bible study class together
Help feed shut-in people
Visit a nursing home

Miscellaneous:

Pillow fight
Visit a pet store
Try on clothes in an exclusive
    store
Go grocery shopping together
Rent a limo for the evening

Go window shopping
Build ice cream sundaes
Babysit together
Do volunteer work together
Have shaving cream fights
Go watch little league games

Test-drive a car
Color coloring books together
Visit the other person's job
Velcro wall jumping (if you
  find one)
Go to an arcade
Do yard work
Rearrange your room(s)
Visit a city that is a name of a state
Go to the airport and watch
  planes take off and land
Read the *Star*, the *Globe*, or
  Enquirer together and laugh
Go watch Jai Alai
See a midnight movie
Thumb wrestling tournament
Take a sleigh ride
Go to a wedding together
Park and starwatch
Drive to and visit Canada
Finger paint
Grocery store replacement
  shopping
Polaroid scavenger hunt

Bus ride to the mall
View a tough man/woman
  competition
Ride a complete city bus trip
Wrestle a wrestling bear
Walk, pet, and love a pet at a
  pet shelter
Visit places significant for
  each other and explain why
Look at Christmas lights
Make musical tapes of
  favorite music
Fruit tree picking/orchard
Go looking for 4 leaf clovers
Draw on a sidewalk with chalk
Go to a stranger's wedding
Jump on a trampoline
Have an innertubing party
Eat hot dogs/sodas at a con-
  venience store
Donate blood
Puddle-jump in the rain
Skip rocks on a lake or pond

Theme Party Dates:

Rocky horror party
Pillow fight party
Hide-and-seek party
Freddy Krueger party
Road rally party
Masquerade party
Smurf party
McDonald's birthday party
Hot-tub party
Superbowl party
Saturday Night Live party

Pie-in-the-face party
M*A*S*H party
Boxer shorts party
K-Mart party (blue light specials)
Cabbage Patch doll cliff-
  diving party
Aliens party
The Fly party
Nuts & bolts party
Twister party
Friday the 13th fest party

Tupperware party
TV shopping-channel party
Chester/Garfield Fest
Christmas in July party
Pumpkin pickin' and carving
  party
Birthday party
Mock wedding
Truth-or-dare party
Bathrobe-and-boxers party
Rotating ethnic dinner party
Shake-the-blues party
Hat 1 = Men Hat 2 = Woman,
  3 = The Date
Bedrock ball bash
Dress as favorite dead person
Coloring books/ crayons
Simpsons party
Clothes-that-clash party
Go on a blind date
Dash for a date: 30 minutes to
  find date
Godfather night
Big-hair party

Match-the-baby-picture party
Secret pal week
Flapjack madness
All-American Party = diff.
  foods, etc.
Different holiday in each
  room party
Go bananas party
T-Shirt graffiti party
Chinese New Year party
I'm-not-Irish St. Paddy's party
American Gladiators party
Come as something you're not
Decorate your car "just mar-
  ried" and drive around and
  count the cars that honk!
Dress as you wannabe party
Monty Python fest party
Biblical characters party
Hollywood star party
Charades party
M.O.R.P. (Backwards Prom)
Grinch party

For Further Reading

Interested in learning more about improving your relationships? We suggest the following books:

The Campus Life Guide to Dating, by Diane Eble. Campus Life Books, Zondervan Publishing House, 1990.

Creative Dating, by Doug Fields and Todd Temple. Oliver Nelson, 1986.

The Lover's Guide to Valentine's Day, Family Digest, Inc., 1993.

Love for a Lifetime: Building a Marriage That Will Go the Distance, by Dr. James Dobson, Multnomah.

Getting to Know You, by Jeanne McSweeney and Charles Leocha. World Leisure Corporation, 1992.

More Than You & Me: Touching Others Through the Strength of Your Marriage, by Kevin and Karen Miller. Focus on the Family.

2002 Things to Do on a Date: The Dating Handbook, by Cyndi Haynes and Dale Edwards. Bob Adams, Inc., 1992.

The Book of Questions: Love and Sex, by Gregory Stock, Ph.D., Workman Publishing, 1989.

52 Dates for You and Your Mate, by Dave and Claudia Arp. Thomas Nelson Publishers, 1993.

Holding on to Romance, by H. Norman Wright. Regal Books, 1992.

Quiet Times for Couples, by H. Norman Wright. Harvest House Publishers, 1990.

Let us hear about your great date! Send a copy of your date 102 to David and Diane Coleman, Coleman Productions, P.O. Box 235, Loveland, OH 45104. Please sign the release below, giving us permission should we wish to include your date among our examples. All names will be changed.

David and Diane Coleman have my permission to use the attached material in their work on dating.

Signature _____

Printed Name _____

Address _____

City_____State _____Zip_____